Niimtoowaad Mikinaag Gijiying Bakonaan
Dancing on Our Turtle's Back

DANCING ON OUR TURTLE'S BACK

STORIES OF NISHNAABEG RE-CREATION,
RESURGENCE AND A NEW EMERGENCE

LEANNE BETASAMOSAKE SIMPSON

ARP BOOKS • WINNIPEG

Copyright ©2011 Leanne Betasamosake Simpson

ARP Books (Arbeiter Ring Publishing)
205-70 Arthur Street
Winnipeg, Manitoba
Treaty 1 Territory and Historic Métis Nation Homeland
Canada R3B 1G7
arpbooks.org

Design by Relish New Brand Experience Inc.
Printed and bound in Canada by Imprimerie Gauvin on certified FSC ® paper
Twelfth printing, January 2023

 Canada Council for the Arts **Conseil des Arts du Canada**  MANITOBA ARTS COUNCIL / CONSEIL DES ARTS DU MANITOBA

 **Canada** **Manitoba**

ARP Books acknowledges the generous support of the Manitoba Arts Council
and the Canada Council for the Arts for our publishing program. We
acknowledge the financial support of the Government of Canada through
the Canada Book Fund and the Province of Manitoba through the Book
Publishing Tax Credit and the Book Publisher Marketing Assistance Program
of Manitoba Culture, Heritage, and Tourism.Library and Archives Canada
Cataloguing in Publication

LIBRARY AND ARCHIVES CANADA CATALOGUING IN PUBLICATION
Simpson, Leanne, 1971-
        Dancing on our turtle's back : stories of Nishnaabeg re-creation,
resurgence, and a new emergence / Leanne Simpson.

Includes bibliographical references.
ISBN 978-1-894037-50-1

        1. Native peoples–Canada–Government relations. 2. Native peoples–
Canada–Politics and government. 3. Native peoples–Canada–Languages–
Revival. I. Title.

E92.S49 2011   323.1197'071   C2011-900594-8

 MIX
Paper
FSC
www.fsc.org   FSC® C100212

For my next generation:
Minowewebeneshiinh, Nishna, Binaakwe,
Aanjinokomi and Mkomiikaa.

GCHI'MIIGWECH

This book was written with support from the Ontario Arts Council and the Canada Council for the Arts, and was completed during a residency at the Leighton Artists' Colony at the Banff Centre. This work was particularly influenced by the oral and written work of Asinykwe (Edna Manitowabi), Gdigaa Migizi (Doug Williams), Robin Greene-ba, Mark Thompson-ba, John Borrows, Wendy Makoons Geniusz, Neal McLeod, Kiera Ladner and the artistic works of Rebecca Belmore. Chi'miigwech to Ursula Pflug for encouraging me to fill out forms, and to Patti Shaughnessy for continuing to organize fabulous and inspiring events in my community.

Edna Manitowabi continues to have a deep and profound influence on my thinking, research and writing. Chi'miigwech to my Elder and friend Edna for her brilliance and power in sharing Nishnaabeg philosophies, traditional stories, language, teachings and songs. Over the past ten years I have learned a tremendous amount from Edna in terms of Nishnaabeg thought, philosophy and values, particularly from the perspectives of women. Edna's teachings have made me into a better Nishnaabekwe. I particularly thank Edna for her contribution "Grandmother Teachings," found in Chapter 2.

Gchi'miigwech to my Elder, teacher, intellectual mentor and friend Gdigaa Migizi (Doug Williams) who spent a great deal of time patiently engaging with me and gently answering my questions. From June to December 2010, we discussed nearly every concept found in this book, and Chapter 3 is very much based on Gdigaa Migizi's knowledge. Gdigaa Migizi's understanding of Michi Saagiig Nishnaabeg philosophy, traditional teachings, language, and intellectual traditions is vast and complex. He has made me into a better Michi Saagiik

Nishnaabekwe. I have tried my best to communicate the essence of both Doug and Edna's teachings in a good way, any mistakes are all mine.

Chi'miigwech to language expert and Elder Shirley Williams who took the time to answer my questions about language and explain to me her understandings of the conceptual meanings encoded in our words. Through Shirley I was able to ground check words used by other Nishnaabeg scholars, words I found in dictionaries and words I learned from other Nishnaabeg. Any mistakes in the language however, are my own.

Chi'miigwech to Kiera Ladner, John Borrows, Christine Sy and Steve Daniels for providing me with feedback on previous drafts of this manuscript. John Borrows spent a good deal of time engaged with the manuscript in an intellectual, philosophical, spiritual and cultural way; and for that I am both honoured and grateful. Kiera provided intelligent and thoughtful insights on the manuscript and a lot of support during the writing phase. Christine provided detailed feedback that made the book better, some of which will require much more thinking.

Thanks also to the Arbeiter Ring collective for their commitment to liberatory politics and of course for continuing to publish Indigenous writing. I could not ask for better allies—particularly John K. Samson who has always believed in my writing and who has been very open and supportive of my work along the way; and Rick Wood for his patience and careful attention to detail. Finally, chi'miigwech to Steve Daniels, the one who accepts me most completely, and to our children Nishna and Minowewebeneshiinh, our greatest teachers.

Miigwech ndi-ninim.

Chapter One

NISHNAABEG¹ RESURGENCE: STORIES FROM WITHIN

On June 21, 2009, a community procession of Michi Saagiig Nishnaabeg² dancers, artists, singers, drummers, community leaders, Elders, families and children walked down the main street of Nogojiwanong.³ With our traditional and contemporary performers gently dancing on the back of our Mikinaag,⁴ we wove our way through the city streets, streets where we had all indirectly, or directly, experienced the violence of colonialism, dispossession and desperation at one time or another. Our drummers provided the heartbeat; our singers provided the prayers. Settler-Canadians poked their heads out of office buildings and stared at us from the sidelines. "Indians. What did they want now? What did they want this time?" But that day, we didn't have any *want*. We were not seeking recognition or asking for rights. We were not trying to fit into Canada. We were celebrating our nation on our lands in the spirit of joy, exuberance and individual expression.

Our allies lined the streets offering smiles and encouraging shouts of approval. Flanked by huge, colourful puppets and a flock of sparkling bineshiinyag⁵ made by local children, the procession was both strikingly disarming and deeply political at the same time. This was not a protest. This was not a demonstration. This was a quiet, collective act of resurgence. It was a mobilization and it was political because it was a reminder. It was a reminder that although we are collectively unseen in the city of Peterborough, when we come together with one mind and one heart we can transform our land and our city into a decolonized space and a place of resurgence, even if it is only for a brief amount of time. It was a reminder of everything good about our traditions, our culture, our songs, dances and performances. It was a celebration of our resistance, a celebration that after everything, we are still here. It was an insertion of Nishnaabeg presence.

As I walked down the main street of the place where I live with my family, I felt a mixture of strong emotions. As I saw my Haudenosaunee and Cree colleagues from the university walking with us, I felt a deepened sense of solidarity. This was a time in my life I felt most connected to my community. But I was also afraid. I was afraid of the response of the non-Natives in my community. I was afraid they would throw things at us, that there would be confrontations, that there would be violence. I was afraid that my kids, having only known joy and beautiful things from their culture, would suddenly have their bubble burst and they would see the violent assault my generation of Indigenous assumes as normal.

The idea of a celebratory community procession is incredible to my eighty-something Nokomis.[6] Growing up on the reserve, and then living in Peterborough, the idea of "Indians" marching down the main street in a celebratory fashion seems fantastical to her at best. She can't believe that her great grandchildren feel proud, that in her words, "It is OK for them to be Indian." And in many ways, that was the point of the procession. The Nishnaabeg have been collectively dispossessed of our national territory; we are an occupied nation. Individually, we have been physically beaten, arrested, apprehended, interned in jails, sanitariums, residential or day schools and foster care. We have endured racist remarks when shopping or seeking healthcare and education within the city. We have stories of being driven to the outskirts of our city by police and bar owners and dropped off to walk back to our reserves. But that day we turned inward to celebrate our presence and to build our resurgence as a community.

For me, it was a beautiful day. I've never walked in solidarity with all of our Nishnaabeg families before, regardless of our individual political orientation. I've never had the opportunity to celebrate our survival, our continuance, our resurgence: all of the best parts of us. For an hour that day, we collectively transformed the streets of Peterborough back into Nogojiwanong, and forward into Nogojiwanong. For an hour that day, we created a space and a place where the impacts of colonialism were lessened, where we could feel what it feels like to be part of a united, healthy community, where our children could glimpse our beautiful visions for their future.

The procession made its way to the shores of Zaagigaans,[7] where we held a Powwow and artistic festival. The cycle of our Grand Entry into the streets of Peterborough was repeated as our Elders and dancers danced their way around the cedar arbor, and we started over once again. Together, we transformed National Aboriginal Day into something about resurgence for our community, instead of a shallow multicultural education day for Canadians to feel less guilty about their continued occupation of our lands. For me, our procession was a political act. We built a day where we put the health of our nation first. We strengthened our culture. We strengthened our relationships with each other and with Nogojiwanong.

Nishnaabe Elder Edna Manitowabi says that one of the reasons our cultures and ways of life are important is that our culture brings our hearts great joy. Our culture is beautiful and loving, and it nurtures our hearts and minds in a way that enables us to not just cope, but to live. We always *feel* good after being out in the bush, or after ceremony. I thought of this that day as I walked. I thought of the word *e-yaa'oyaanh*, which means who I am, the way I am living or becoming, my identity.[8] In order to have a positive identity we have to be living in ways that illuminate that identity, and that propel us towards mino bimaadiziwin, the good life.[9]

Gaawiin Nda-gajsii, We Are Not Shameful

For most of the day, I thought about my Ancestors. I thought of the seeds they had planted so long ago to ensure that we were all there on that day in June, walking down our street together. And if I am honest, I also thought of the shame that I carry inside of me from the legacy of colonial abuse, the unspoken shame we carry collectively as Michi Saagiig Nishnaabeg. It is shame that is rooted in the humiliation that colonialism has heaped on our peoples for hundreds of years and is now carried within our bodies, minds and our hearts. It is shame that our ancestors—our families—did not rally hard enough against the colonial regime. It is shame that we were tricked into surrendering our life, land and sustenance during the Williams Treaty process. It is shame that makes us think that our leaders and Elders did not do the best they could. To me, this colonial shame felt like not only a tremendous burden to carry, but it also felt displaced. We are not shameful people. We have done nothing wrong. I began to realize that shame can only take hold when we are disconnected from the stories of resistance within our own families and communities. I placed that shame as an insidious and infectious part of the cognitive imperialism that was aimed at convincing us that we were a weak and defeated people, and that there was no point in resisting or resurging. I became interested in finding those stories of resistance and telling them so that our next generation would know.

I was recently in the community of Kahnesatà:ke for the twentieth anniversary commemoration of the "Oka Crisis." The day was intensely emotional as community members shared their memories and trauma of the crisis and its aftermath. At one point during the day, Ellen Gabriel, who had been the spokesperson for the People of the Pines during the summer of 1990, stood up and simply said, "We have nothing to be ashamed of. We have done nothing wrong." Her statement echoed through the crowd of mostly community members; there was not a dry eye in the room. I echo Ellen's words. We have nothing to be ashamed of, and we have done nothing wrong.

Michi Saagiig Nishnaabeg territory is located along the north shore of Lake Ontario, or Chi'Nbiish,[10] from Niagara Falls to Gananoque. Our old people referred to our nation as Kina Gchi Nishnaabegogaming: *Kina* meaning all; *Gchi* for big; and *ogamig* meaning the place of, where we live, where we make our living, the place that was given to us.[11] Our oral tradition tells of a beautiful territory covered with mature stands of white pine with trunks spanning seven feet and towering 200 feet overhead. The land was easy to travel through, with pine needles and a sparse understory as a result of a white pine canopy. There was a tall grass prairie where Peterborough stands today—a prairie that the Michi Saagiig Nishnaabeg maintained with controlled burns.[12] It's hard for me to imagine a land like that today, with southeastern Ontario farmland spanning out in all directions.

For my ancestors, the Michi Saagiig Nishnaabeg, our self-determination and sovereignty as part of the Nishnaabeg nation was relatively intact between 1700–1783.[13] Over the next forty years we were forced to survive an intense, violent assault on our lands and our peoples. By 1763, the British Crown no longer needed us as allies; soon loyalists streamed into our territory and began occupying Michi Saagiig Nishnaabeg lands. Over the next fifty years, our people survived pandemics, violence and assault, unjust treaty negotiations, occupation of our lands, and a forced relocation—which, for some of us, resulted in a small and insufficient reserve at Alderville, a Methodist mission. Eventually our system of governance was replaced by a colonial administration, as the planned assimilation strategy moved into full swing. By 1822—when many Nishnaabeg in the north and the west were still living as they always had—we were facing the complete political, cultural and social collapse of everything we had ever known.

My ancestors resisted and survived what must have seemed like an apocalyptic reality of occupation and subjugation in a context where they had few choices. They resisted by simply surviving and being alive. They resisted by holding onto their stories They resisted by taking the seeds of our culture and political systems and packing them away, so that one day another generation of Michi Saagiig Nishnaabeg might be able to plant them. I am sure of their resistance, because I am here today, living as a contemporary Michi Saagiig Nishnaabeg woman. I am the evidence. Michi Saagiig Nishnaabeg people are the evidence. Now, nearly two hundred years after surviving an attempted political and cultural genocide, it is the responsibility of my generation to plant and nurture those seeds and to make our Ancestors proud.

Shame traps us individually and collectively into the victimry of the colonial assault, and travels through the generations, accumulating and manifesting itself in new and more insidious ways in each re-generation. The cycles of shame we are cognitively locked into is in part perpetuated and maintained by western theoretical constructions of "resistance," "mobilization" and "social movements," by defining what is and is not considered. Through the lens of colonial thought and cognitive imperialism, we are often unable to *see* our Ancestors. We are unable to *see* their philosophies and their strategies of mobilization and the complexities of their plan for resurgence. When resistance is defined solely as large-scale political mobilization, we miss much of what has kept our languages, cultures, and systems of governance alive. We have those things today because our Ancestors often acted within the family unit to physically survive, to pass on what they could to their children, to occupy and use our lands as we always had. This, in and of itself, tells me a lot about how to build Indigenous renaissance and resurgence.

A Flourishment of the Indigenous Inside

Social movement theory is one of the primary academic sites of theorizing political mobilization. There are few comprehensive critiques of social movement theory by Indigenous Peoples, yet it is telling that few Indigenous scholars use this approach to explain Indigenous resistance and mobilization.[14] Social movement theory is, for the most part, inadequate in explaining the forces that generate and propel Indigenous resistance and resurgence because it is rooted in western knowledge and a western worldview, ignoring Indigenous political culture and theory. Social movement theory also ignores the historical context of Indigenous resistance—spanning over 400 years for some Indigenous nations—by disregarding differences in political organization, governance and political cultures between Canadian and Indigenous societies. At their core, Indigenous political movements contest the very foundation of the Canadian state in its current expression, while most theories of group politics and social movements take the state for granted.[15] Defining and analyzing Indigenous resurgence from a social movement perspective erroneously concludes that there has not yet been an Indigenous social movement in Canada,[16] a conclusion that flies in the face of 400 years of Indigenous resistance. We have been resisting colonial imposition for four centuries. I think our communities know something about organizing, mobilizing and strategizing. I think our communities know quite a lot about *living* through the most grievous of circumstances.

Although I have been thinking about resistance for my entire adult life, it was not until I read Taiaiake Alfred's *Peace, Power and*

Righteousness: An Indigenous Manifesto and then *Wasáse: Indigenous Pathways of Action and Freedom*, that I began to think about resurgence. Alfred's seminal works immediately spoke to my *(o)debwewin*, literally the sound my heart makes,[7] or "truth," because at the core of his work, he challenges us to reclaim the *Indigenous* contexts (knowledge, interpretations, values, ethics, processes) for our political cultures. In doing so, he refocuses our work from trying to transform the colonial outside into a flourishment of the *Indigenous* inside. We need to rebuild our culturally inherent philosophical contexts for governance, education, healthcare, and economy. We need to be able to articulate in a clear manner our visions for the future, for living as *Indigenous Peoples* in contemporary times. To do so, we need to engage in *Indigenous* processes, since according to our traditions, the processes of engagement highly influence the outcome of the engagement itself. We need to do this on our own terms, without the sanction, permission or engagement of the state, western theory or the opinions of Canadians. In essence, we need to not just figure out who we are; we need to re-establish the processes by which we live who we are within the current context we find ourselves. We do not need funding to do this. We do not need a friendly colonial political climate to do this. We do not need opportunity to do this. We need our Elders, our languages, and our lands, along with vision, intent, commitment, community and ultimately, action. We must move ourselves beyond resistance and survival, to flourishment and mino bimaadiziwin.[18] If this approach does nothing else to shift the current state of affairs—and I believe it will—it will ground our peoples in their own cultures and teachings that provide the ultimate antidote to colonialism, which I believe is what Indigenous intellectuals and theorists[19] have been encouraging us to do all along. In this book, I am interested in exploring these transformative contexts from within my own Nishnaabeg culture. Transforming ourselves, our communities and our nations is ultimately the first step in transforming our relationship with the state.

Building diverse, nation-culture-based resurgences means significantly re-investing in our own ways of being: regenerating our political and intellectual traditions; articulating and living our legal systems; language learning; ceremonial and spiritual pursuits; creating and

using our artistic and performance-based traditions. All of these require us—as individuals and collectives—to diagnose, interrogate
and eviscerate the insidious nature of conquest, empire, and imperial
thought in every aspect of our lives. It requires us to reclaim the very
best practices of our traditional cultures, knowledge systems and lifeways in the dynamic, fluid, compassionate, respectful context within
which they were originally generated. A critical level of anti-colonial
interrogation is required in order for us to be able to see the extraordinarily political nature of Nishnaabeg thought.

Ethically, it is my emphatic belief that the land, reflected in
Nishnaabeg thought and philosophy, compels us towards resurgence
in virtually every aspect. Walking through the bush last spring with
my children, the visual landscape reminded me of this. We saw Lady
Slippers, and I was reminded of our name for the flower and the story
that goes with it,[20] and then moss, and then butterflies.[21] Then we saw
a woodpecker[22] and I thought of a similar story. Finally, we walked
through a birch stand and I thought of Nanabush, Niimkiig and
birch bark.[23] Our Nishnaabeg landscape flourishes with our stories of
resistance and resurgence, yet through colonial eyes, the stories are
interpreted as quaint anecdotes with "rules" of engagement and con-
sequence. Interpreted within our cultural web of non-authoritarian
leadership, non-hierarchical ways of being, non-interference and non-
essentialism,[24] the stories explain the resistance of my Ancestors and
the seeds of resurgence they so carefully saved and planted. So I could
then assume my responsibility as a Michi Saagiig Nishnaabeg to care
take of their garden, eventually passing those responsibilities on to my
grandchildren. This is the purpose of this book.

While it is my firm belief that there is much work to be done
within our nations in terms of building resurgence—both political
and cultural—within a nation-based framework, I don't believe this
is *all* we need to do. According to our Seven Fires Prophecy, much
work needs to be done to decolonize the state, Indigenous-state relations and Canada in order for the Eighth Fire to be lit.[25] At this point,
to me, it seems rather futile to be engaged in scholarly and political
processes, trying to shift these relationships when there is no evidence
there exists the political will to do so on the part of the Canadian state.

There is no opportunity; and putting our energies into demanding that
the state recognize us seems depressing, futile and a waste of energy,
given the condition of our communities. I also believe Nishnaabeg
philosophy propels us to focus on ourselves in terms of transformation.
However, I do not wish to criticize the work of Indigenous academics who chose to engage, interrogate and struggle with the dominant white paper liberalism that plagues Indigenous-state relations in
Canada. The seminal works of many of my colleagues are at their core
aimed at decolonizing the Canadian state, political systems and legal
system in order to demand political relationships based on recognized
Indigenous nations and alternatives to rights-based approaches. While
this body of work searches for solutions within federalism that do
not subsume Indigenous self-determination, agency and sovereignty,
there is also important work to be done within our nations. This is
the work that is the focus of this book, because these are the things
that I am constantly thinking about, talking about, and asking Elders
about. My approach to this work is not rooted solely in the intellectual; it is rooted in my spiritual and emotional life, as well as my body;
and it is explored through my Nishnaabeg name, my clan, my Michi
Saagiig Nishnaabeg roots and my own individual being. It is not better
or worse than any other Michi Saagiig Nishnaabeg's contribution. It
is simply a reflection of my own current ideas and thinking and is not
meant to reflect the views of my broader nation, or to be comprehensive in any manner.

   In my own life, I have been taught by a handful of Elders that embody Nishnaabeg thought in a way that I worry we are losing. These
Elders are fluent language speakers. They embody gentleness and
kindness. And what struck me immediately—and continues to do
so twenty years later—is that they rejected rigidity and fundamentalism as colonial thinking. Their ways of being in the world and their
interpretations of our teachings were reflective of a philosophical
state, a set of values and ethics and a way of being in the world where
they didn't feel the need to employ exclusionary practices, authoritarian power and hierarchy. They "protected" their interpretations
by embodying them and by living them. They "resisted" colonialism by living within Nishnaabeg contexts. When I moved back into

the southeastern regions of my territory, I was immediately struck by moralistic judgment, rules to constrict and control social behaviours within my community, and a more formalized hierarchy to restrict access to knowledge, which to me is reminiscent of colonial thought and religious fundamentalism.[26] This was not my understanding or interpretation of my own cultural teachings. I was taught that individual Nishnaabe had the responsibility of interpreting the teachings for themselves within a broader shared collective set of values that placed great importance on self-actualization, the suspension of judgment, fluidity, emergence, careful deliberation and an embodied respect for diversity.

There exists very little in the academic literature conceptualizing and exploring resistance and resurgence from within Indigenous thought.[27] My perspective throughout this book is that the process of resurgence must be Indigenous at its core in order to reclaim and re-politicize the context and the nature of Nishnaabeg thought. Nishnaabeg thought was designed and conceptualized to perpetuate the holistic well being of Nishnaabeg people through a series of cultural and political manifestations, including government, education, and restorative justice that promoted mino bimaadiziwin. Our ways of being promoted the good life or continuous rebirth at every turn: in the face of political unrest, "natural disasters" and even genocide. Nishnaabeg thought provides us with the impetus, the ethical responsibility, the strategies and the plan of action for resurgence. We have a responsibility to the coming generations to maintain that resurgence in the midst of an all-out colonial attack and in the more insidious decentralized post-colonial-colonialism.[28] Nishnaabeg thought was not meant to promote assimilation or normalization within a colonial context. It was not meant to be reduced and relegated to a decorative window dressing in western scholarship.

Aanji Maajitaawin,[29] the Art of Starting Over

I am writing this at a time when Canada is busy talking about "reconciliation" at every turn, while at the same time using the *Indian Act* to enforce a band council "government" against the will of the

Algonquins of Barriere Lake. "Reconciliation" is being promoted by the federal government as a "new" way for Canada to relate to Indigenous Peoples, and it isn't just government officials that are promoting the idea. I have heard heads of universities talk about reconciliation; I have read journalist's op-ed pieces; I have heard mayors talk about reconciliation as they open local Aboriginal events. But the idea of reconciliation is not new. Indigenous Peoples attempted to reconcile our differences in countless treaty negotiations, which categorically have not produced the kinds of relationships Indigenous Peoples intended. I wonder how we can reconcile when the majority of Canadians do not understand the historic or contemporary injustice of dispossession and occupation, particularly when the state has expressed its unwillingness to make any adjustments to the unjust relationship. Haudenosaunee scholar and orator Dan Longboat recently reminded me of this, when he said that treaties are not just for governments, they are for the citizens as well.[30] The people also have to act in a manner that is consistent with the relationships set out in the treaty negotiation process. If Canadians do not fully understand and embody the idea of reconciliation, is this a step forward? It reminds me of an abusive relationship where one person is being abused physically, emotionally, spiritually and mentally. She wants out of the relationship, but instead of supporting her, we are all gathered around the abuser, because he wants to "reconcile." But he doesn't want to take responsibility. He doesn't want to change. In fact, all through the process he continues to physically, emotionally, spiritually and mentally abuse his partner. He just wants to say sorry so he can feel less guilty about his behaviour. He just wants to adjust the ways he is abusing; he doesn't want to stop the abuse. Collectively, what are the implications of participating in reconciliation processes when there is an overwhelming body of evidence that in action, the Canadian state does not want to take responsibility and stop the abuse? What are the consequences for Indigenous Peoples of participating in a process that attempts to absolve Canada of past wrong doings, while they continue to engage with our nations in a less than honourable way?

Those that chose to participate in reconciliation processes do so believing that participation could potentially bring more positive change than non-participation. They may be right. But our eyes need to be wide open if we are entering this process. As reconciliation has become institutionalized,[31] I worry our participation will benefit the state in an asymmetrical fashion, by attempting to neutralize the legitimacy of Indigenous resistance. If reconciliation is focused only on residential schools rather than the broader set of relationships that generated policies, legislation and practices aimed at assimilation and political genocide, then there is a risk that reconciliation will "level the playing field" in the eyes of Canadians. In the eyes of liberalism, the historical "wrong" has now been "righted" and further transformation is not needed, since the historic situation has been remedied. I worry the historical context for contemporary Indigenous-state contention becomes co-opted in this model, because the perception of most Canadians is that post-reconciliation, Indigenous Peoples no longer have a legitimate source of contention.[32] I also worry that institutionalization of a narrowly defined "reconciliation" subjugates treaty and nation-based participation by locking our Elders—the ones that suffered the most directly at the hands of the residential school system—in a position of victimhood. Of course, they are anything but victims. They are our strongest visionaries and they inspire us to vision alternative futures. Are we participating in a process that allows the state to co-opt the individual and collective pain and suffering of our people, while also criminalizing the inter-generational impacts of residential schools and ignoring the larger neo-assimilation project to which our children are now subjected?

For reconciliation to be meaningful to Indigenous Peoples and for it to be a decolonizing force, it must be interpreted broadly. To me, reconciliation must be grounded in cultural generation and political resurgence. It must support Indigenous nations in regenerating our languages, our oral cultures, our traditions of governance and everything else residential schools attacked and attempted to obliterate.[33] Reconciliation must move beyond individual abuse to come to mean a collective re-balancing of the playing field. This idea is captured in the Nishnaabeg concept *Aanji Maajitaawin*: to start over, the art of starting over, to regenerate. Reconciliation is a process of regeneration that will take many years to accomplish. We have to regenerate our languages so we have communities of fluent speakers. We have to regenerate the conditions that produce leaders and political systems based on our collective Nishnaabeg values, political processes and philosophies. Canada must engage in a decolonization project and a re-education project that would enable its government and its citizens to engage with Indigenous Peoples in a just and honourable way in the future.

From a Nishnaabeg theoretical and legal perspective, regeneration or restoration is at the core of re-balancing relationships. Nishnaabeg legal systems are, at their core, restorative. Restorative processes rely upon the abuser taking full responsibility for his/her actions in a collective setting, amongst the person s/he violated, and amongst the people both the perpetrator and the survivor hold responsibilities to—be that their extended family, clan, or community. In the case of state-perpetuated residential schools, the tables would be turned in a Nishnaabeg legal system. The survivors would have agency, decision-making power, and the power to decide restorative measures. In the case of the Community Holistic Circles of Healing in Hollow Water First Nation,[34] the abuser must take responsibility for his or her actions and is required to sit in a circle of community Elders, the extended family of the survivor, and his or her extended family (who are there to support him or her through this process. Everyone participating in the circle has a chance to speak or to share their thoughts, feelings and perspectives. The survivor has the choice to share whatever he or she feels most appropriate. Imagine government officials, church officials, nuns, priests and teachers from a particular residential school in a circle with the people that had survived their sexual, physical, emotional and spiritual abuse. This is a fundamentally different power relationship between perpetrators of violence and survivors of that violence, where the abusers must face the full impact of their actions. Reconciliation then becomes a process embodied by both the survivor and the perpetrator. And part of restoration means that the community maintains the authority to make that individual accountable for future wrongs. The interrogation is focused on the perpetrator of the violence, not on the survivors. The responsibility and the authority for restoration are in the agency of the survivors, not the perpetrators themselves. The authority to hold the state accountable then rests with Indigenous nations, not the liberal state.[35]

Restorative models work in Nishnaabeg communities because ethically taking responsibility for one's actions is paramount in the healing or restoration process; as well, the purpose of these models in the long term is the rehabilitation and restoration of all of those individuals back into mino bimaadiziwin. These models put the hens in charge of the hen house and the fox under interrogation. If it is truly time to talk "reconciliation," then how we reconcile is critically important. I can see no evidence whatsoever that there exists a political will on the part of the state to do anything other than neutralize Indigenous resistance, so as to not impinge upon the convenience of the settler-Canadians. The only way to not be co-opted is to use our own legal and political processes to bring about justice.

In the words of Dene scholar Glen Coulthard, our culturally inherent political theory provides Indigenous Peoples with mechanisms for "critically revaluating, reconstructing and redeploying culture and tradition in ways that seek to prefigure, alongside those with similar ethical commitments, a radical alternative to the structural and psycho-affective facets of colonial domination."[36] Our liberatory and inherent theories of resurgence also do not tell us to persistently search through the web of colonial traps for settler political recognition and to gleefully accept white paper liberalism designed to redistribute resources and rights, placating the guilt of settler Canadians and neutralizing Indigenous resistance. Our inherent theories of resurgence are transformative and revolutionary. They are meant to propel and maintain social, cultural and political transformative movement through the worst forms of political genocide; and I think it is important to understand them as such.

While there are Indigenous scholars, leaders and activists engaged in broadening the state's conceptualization of reconciliation in order to re-align it with the political goals of Indigenous Peoples, again, I worry about emphasis. This cannot become the bulk of our work or take up the bulk of our resources. Perhaps good things will come out of this process, particularly for residential school survivors. Perhaps our communities will be able to use something from this "reconciliation process" to meet some of their goals, but we need to enter into this carefully and with critical eyes that are guided by the whole picture.

What follows in this book is the beginning of an exploration of the theoretical foundations of resurgence and regeneration from within Nishnaabeg political and intellectual traditions. I have been careful throughout this chapter and the book to not define "resurgence." It is my hope that readers will take the concepts and ideas presented in this book, return to their own communities, teachings, languages and Elders or Knowledge Holders and to engage in a process where they figure out what "resurgence" means to them, and to their collective communities. This book is what resurgence means to me, at this point in my life. And while this is a personal process, I believe it is also important to collectivize these discussions and processes. In sharing my thoughts on this, my hope is that readers will take what is useful to them and illuminate it in their lives and their work, while leaving the parts that they disagree with to die within the pages of the book. I know my thinking on this will change, because the process I am engaged with is transformative. As my language skills increase, so will my thinking. As I move through different stages in my life, so will my thinking.

In our ceremonies, we have a beautiful and sacred Nishnaabeg song, commonly referred to as our Prophecy Song. My understanding is that the Prophecy Song is very, very ancient.[37] The grammatical structure is such that it is the voices and words of our Ancestors as the beginning of the Seven Fires Prophecy, singing encouragement to the coming generations who are responsible for building a Nishnaabeg resurgence in the Seventh Fire. The song is an incredible gift from my Ancestors. It is a song of resistance and resurgence; and when we sing it, its haunting melody fills our hearts with hope, with love, with beauty and thanksgiving. It is a single song that has the power to liberate us from shame. Aambe Maajaadaa![38]

---

1   *Nishnaabeg* is translated as "the people" and refers to Ojibwe, Odawa (Ottawa), Potawatomi, Michi Saagiig (Mississauga), Saulteaux, Chippewa and Omámíwinini (Algonquin) people. Nishnaabeg people are also known as Nishinaabeg, Anishinaabeg, Anishinaabek, and Anishinabek, reflecting different spelling systems and differing dialects. I have used many Nishnaabemowin (Ojibwe language) words throughout this book, and I have used the dialects of

the people who taught me the words. The words I learned from Doug Williams are in the Michi Saagiig Nishnaabeg or eastern Ontario dialect. Shirley Williams and Isadore Toulouse speak Odawa or the central/Manitoulin dialect. There are also a few words in the northwestern dialect. I am a language learner, not a fluent speaker, and any mistakes are my own. I have, however, tried to check each word that is unfamiliar to me with an Elder who is a fluent language speaker to ensure that I am using the word correctly, even if the word is coming from a reputable dictionary. In Michi Saagiig Nishnaabeg contexts, I have tried to use our spelling—Nishnaabe or Nishnaabeg (plural), when referring to the work of other writers from the northwest parts of our territory. I have used the spelling they use in their work. Because there are too many examples of academics who are not fluent speakers using Nishnaabemowin words incorrectly, I have referenced all but the most common Nishnaabemowin words in the text.

2   *Michi Saagiig Nishnaabeg* means the Nishnaabeg people who live or dwell at the mouth of a large river. Michi Saagiig Nishnaabeg Elder Doug Williams explained to me that this is the way his Elders referred to themselves. Peterborough, ON, October 26, 2010. This is similar to Basil Johnston's Mizhi-zaugeek, *Anishinaubae Thesaurus*, Michigan State University Press, East Lansing, MI, 2006, 14. Michi Saagiig or "Mizhi-zaugeek" people live at the eastern doorway of the Nishnaabeg nation, located in what is now known as eastern Ontario. According to Doug Williams, the word "Mississauga" is an anglicized version of Michi Saagiig or Mizhi-zaugeek.

3   *Nogojiwanong* is the Michi Saagiig name for Peterborough, Ontario, and means "the place at the end of the rapids." It is commonly used amongst Nishnaabeg people in Peterborough.

4   Turtle.

5   Birds.

6   Grandmother.

7   This is the name for Little Lake and it means "little lake." I learned this word from Doug Williams. Waawshkigaamagki (Curve Lake First Nation), July 15, 2010. Shirley Williams showed me how to spell it. Peterborough, ON, September 20, 2010.

8   To me this word means that in order to have a Nishnaabeg identity, one must live that identity in all of its many and beautiful diverse forms. The spelling and full meaning of this word was taught to me by Shirley Williams. Peterborough, ON, September 19, 2010.

9   The art of living the good life. Winona LaDuke also translates mino bimaadiziwin to mean "continuous rebirth." Scott Lyons writes that we should use the bimadizi form of the word to keep with the verb-based traditions of the language. Language expert Shirley Williams translates *bimadizi* to mean he/she is living, and *bimaadiziwin* as an abstract noun meaning "the art of living life." Peterborough, ON, September 12, 2010. As a concept, mino bimaadiziwin is commonly used in Nishnaabeg teachings. I worry though that it is becoming almost an overused and over simplified concept in Nishnaabeg scholarship

particularly amongst non-speakers and cultural beginners (Christine Sy also brought up this point in previous drafts). While I still find mino bimaadiziwin to be an important concept, I use it while keeping these observations in mind.

10   *Chi'Nbiish*, literally "big water," is the Michi Saagiig Nishnaabeg name for Lake Ontario, according to Doug Williams. Peterborough, ON, November 30, 2010.

11   Doug Williams. Peterborough, ON, November 30, 2010. I specifically asked Doug if there was a term our ancestors used to refer to their "nation," and this was his response. My interest in this came out of a conversation with Niigaanwewidam James Sinclair that took place in November 2010.

12   Doug Williams, Keynote Speaker. Peterborough Race Relations Committee, Dreams of Beans Coffee House, Peterborough, ON, November 18, 2010.

13   Brian Osborne and Michael Ripmeester, "The Mississaugas Between Two Worlds: Strategic Adjustments to Changing Landscapes of Power," *Canadian Journal of Native Studies*, 1997, XVII(2): 259–291.

14   Kiera L. Ladner, "*Aysaka'paykinit*: Contesting the Rope Around the Nations' Neck," in Miriam Smith, ed., *Group Politics and Social Movements in Canada*, Broadview Press, Peterborough, ON, 2008, 244.

15   Kiera L. Ladner, "*Aysaka'paykinit*: Contesting the Rope Around the Nations' Neck," in Miriam Smith, ed., *Group Politics and Social Movements in Canada*, Broadview Press, Peterborough, ON, 2008, 228.

16   Rima Wilkes, "The Protest Actions of Indigenous Peoples: A Canadian-U.S. Comparison of Social Movement Emergence," *American Behavioral Scientist*, 2007, 50(4): 510–525.

17   Jim Dumont, Nishnaabeg Elder. Explained in a workshop as part of his presentation at the Elders' Conference, Trent University, Peterborough, ON, February 20, 2010.

18   Mino bimaadiziwin is a phrase that is used to denote "living the good life" or "the art of living the good life." Winona LaDuke translates the term as "continuous rebirth," (Winona LaDuke, *Our Relations: Struggles for Land and Life*, South End Press, Cambridge, MA, 1994, 4, 132), so it means living life in a way that promotes rebirth, renewal, reciprocity and respect. It is my understanding that although there are many ways to live the good life and that within Nishnaabeg contexts, there is no dichotomy between the "good life" and the "bad life," rather living in a good way is an ongoing process. This will become clear later in the book.

19   By here I mean Elders, Faith-Keepers, Clan-Mothers, traditional leaders, Grandmothers, Grandfathers, language-keepers and Knowledge-Holders, not western-trained academics, and I specifically mean those Elders, Faith-Keepers, Clan-Mothers, traditional leaders, Grandmothers, Grandfathers, language-keepers and Knowledge Holders that are able to interpret our teachings through the language in a way that embodies their Nishnaabeg essence, rather than in a way that locks us into a fundamentalist preservation framework.

20   For a written version of this story, see Lise Lunge-Larsen and Margi Preus, *The Legend of the Lady Slipper*, Houghton Mifflin, 1999.

21   One version of this story exists in "The First Butterflies" in *Tales the Elders Told: Ojibway Legends* by Basil Johnston, Royal Ontario Museum, Toronto ON, 1983, 12–17; another exists in John Borrows' *Drawing Out Law: A Spirit's Guide*, University of Toronto Press, Toronto, ON, 2010, 14–16.

22   Basil Johnston, "The Woodpecker" in *The Bear-Walker and Other Stories*, Royal Ontario Museum, Toronto, ON, 1983, 49–55.

23   *Niimkiig* means thunderbirds. For a version of this story see Wendy Makoons Geniusz's "Nenabozho and the Animkikiig" in *Our Knowledge is Not Primitive: Decolonizing Botanical Anishinaabeg Teachings*, Syracuse University Press, Syracuse NY, 2009, 136–140.

24   Kiera Ladner, "Women and Blackfoot Nationalism," *Journal of Canadian Studies* 2000, 35(2): 35–61; Rupert Ross, *Dancing with a Ghost: Exploring Indian Reality*, Reed Books Canada, Markham, ON, 1992, 11–38, 116–125; and Emma LaRoque, "Métis and Feminist" in *Making Space for Indigenous Feminism*, Joyce Green, ed., Fernwood Publishing, Halifax, NS, 2007, 63.

25   For a broader discussion, see Leanne Betasamosake Simpson, "Oshkimaadiziig, the New People," in Leanne Betasamosake Simpson, ed., *Lighting the Eighth Fire: The Liberation, Resurgence, and Protection of Indigenous Nations*, Arbeiter Ring Publishing, Winnipeg, MB, 2008, 13–21.

26   This exists in all parts of the territory; this is just how I came to understand it. Compare this section with Taiaiake Alfred, *Wasáse: Indigenous Pathways of Action and Freedom*, Broadview Press, Peterborough, ON, 2005, 197-8. I have also discussed my observations with Doug Williams, which he felt were consistent with Michi Saagiig Nishnaabeg interpretations. Waawshkigaamagki (Curve Lake First Nation), July 15, 2010.

27   Leanne Betasamosake Simpson, "Oshkimaadiziig, the New People," in Leanne Betasamosake Simpson, ed., *Lighting the Eighth Fire: The Liberation, Resurgence, and Protection of Indigenous Nations*, Arbeiter Ring Publishing, Winnipeg, MB, 2008, 13–21. Alfred explores these concepts within Haudenosaunee thought in Taiaiake Alfred, *Wasáse: Indigenous Pathways of Action and Freedom*, Broadview Press, Peterborough, ON, 2005.

28   Taiaiake Alfred, *Wasáse: Indigenous Pathways of Action and Freedom*, Broadview Press, Peterborough, ON, 2005, 58.

29   *Aanji maajitaawin* means to start over, the art of starting over, or regeneration. Shirley Williams, Peterborough, ON, September 19, 2010.

30   Haudenosaunee scholar Roronhiakewen Dan Longboat, Peterborough, ON, September 9, 2010.

31   I recognize that this discussion is delicate in that I do not want to offend or disregard the experiences, thoughts and perspectives of residential school survivors, nor is it my intent to criticize my colleagues who are working with the Truth and Reconciliation Commission. My intent here is to examine the wider political forces shaping this process of reconciliation.

32 I wrote this while listening to (and was influenced by) Fiona MacDonald's oral presentation, *Democratic Multinationalism: A Political Approach to Indigenous-State Relations in Canada*, Canadian Political Science Association Annual Meeting, June 3, Concordia University, Montreal, QC.

33 This idea came out of a discussion with Kiera Ladner on August 15, 2010.

34 A description of Hollow Water First Nation's Community Holistic Circle Healing is available at <www.iirp.org/article_detail.php?article_id=NDco>. I have worked with the community of Hollow Water since 1997 and have witnessed several CHCH circles.

35 I recognize here that survivors may not want to face their abusers in this fashion. My point here is to bring attention to the shift in power and emphasis in Indigenous restorative processes.

36 Glen S. Coulthard, "Subjects of Empire," *Contemporary Political Theory*, 2007 (6): 437–460.

37 My understanding is my own interpretation of the teachings of Edna Manitowabi who initially shared the song with me, and explained its meaning. Stoney Lake, ON, December 14, 2010.

38 The first line of the song is "Aambe Maajaadaa!," literally "Come On! Let's get going!"

Chapter Two

THEORIZING RESURGENCE FROM WITHIN NISHNAABEG THOUGHT[39]

One of the most crucial tasks presently facing Indigenous nations is the continued creation of individuals and assemblages of people who can think in culturally inherent ways. By this I mean ways that reflect the diversity of thought within our broader cosmologies, those very ancient ways that are inherently counter to the influences of colonial hegemony. I believe we need intellectuals who can think within the conceptual meanings of the language, who are intrinsically connected to place and territory, who exist in the world as an embodiment of contemporary expressions of our ancient stories and traditions, and that illuminate mino bimaadiziwin in all aspect of their lives.

Western theory, whether based in post-colonial, critical or even liberatory strains of thought, has been exceptional at diagnosing, revealing and even interrogating colonialism; and many would argue that this body of theory holds the greatest promise for shifting the Canadian politic because it speaks to that audience in a language they can understand, if not hear. Yet western theories of liberation have for the most part failed to resonate with the vast majority of Indigenous Peoples, scholars or artists. In particularly, western-based social movement theory has failed to recognize the broader contextualizations of resistance within Indigenous thought, while also ignoring the contestation of colonialism as a starting point. While I believe liberatory theory and politics are always valuable, Indigenous thought has the ability to resonate with Indigenous Peoples of all ages. It not only maps a way out of colonial thinking by confirming Indigenous lifeways or alternative ways of being in the world. Ultimately Indigenous theory seeks to dismantle colonialism while simultaneously building a renaissance of mino bimaadiziwin. What if this was our collective focus?

Part of being Indigenous in the 21st century is that regardless of where or how we have grown up, we've all been bathed in a vat of cognitive imperialism, perpetuating the idea that Indigenous Peoples were not, and are not, thinking peoples—an insidious mechanism to promote neo-assimilation and obfuscate the historic atrocities of colonialism.[40] In both subtle and overt ways, the current generation of Indigenous Peoples has been repeatedly told that individually we are stupid, and that collectively our nations were and are void of higher thought. This is reinforced when the academic industrial complex— often propped up by Indian and Northern Affairs Canada (INAC)—promotes colonizing education to our children and youth as the solution to dispossession, poverty, violence and a lack of self-determination over our lives. Cognitive imperialism also rears its ugly head in every discipline every time a student is told that there is no literature or no thinking available on any given topic from within Indigenous intellectual traditions.

Our Elders and Knowledge Holders have always put great emphasis into *how* things are done. This reinforces the idea that it is our own tools, strategies, values, processes and intellect that are going to build our new house. While theoretically, we have debated whether Audre Lourde's "the master's tools can dismantle the master's house," I am interested in a different question. I am not so concerned with how we dismantle the master's house, that is, which sets of theories we use to critique colonialism; but I am very concerned with how we (re)build our own house, or our own houses. I have spent enough time taking down the master's house, and now I want most of my energy to go into visioning and building our new house.

For me, this discussion begins with our Creation Stories, because these stories set the "theoretical framework," or give us the ontological context from within which we can interpret other stories, teachings and experiences.[41] These stories and their Nishnaabeg context are extremely important to our way of being; and they are told and retold in our communities throughout one's life. Our children first start to learn Nishnaabeg thought and theory through these Aandisokaanan[42] very early in their lives. As they travel through the Four Hills of Life,[43] these teachings deepen and resonate in different ways. Benton-Banai writes:

> "And so, Anishinaabe can see that if he knows his creation story, if she knows her creation story, they know also how all of life moves. They can know how life comes to be. All of life is a creative process that began in this original way and continues in the same way in all aspects of our life. In all places and all facets of creation, and creative activity, these seven stages are reflected."[44]

Our Elders tell us that everything we need to know is encoded in the structure, content and context of these stories and the relationships, ethics and responsibilities required to *be* our own Creation Story. In my own life, I did not fully understand this story until I became pregnant with my first child. My Elder Edna Manitowabi guided me through my pregnancy, revealing the responsibilities that go along with bringing forth new life, with nurturing that life with my own sacred water, my thoughts, my emotions, my breath, and my own creative power. In doing so, Edna breathed into me a new way of seeing the world and of being in it. So for me, this is the only place to begin.

Gwiinmaagemi Gdi-dbaajimowinaanin, We Tell Stories

Cree scholar, poet and visual artist Neal McLeod has written extensively about the importance of storytelling in his book *Cree Narrative Memory: From Treaties to Contemporary Times*. Neal writes that the process of storytelling within Cree traditions requires storytellers to remember the ancient stories that made their ancestors "the people they were," and that this requires a remembering of language. He also emphasizes that storytellers have a responsibility to the future to imagine a social space that is just and where Cree narratives will flourish.[45] Storytelling is at its core decolonizing, because it is a process of remembering, visioning and creating a just reality where Nishnaabeg live as both *Nishnaabeg* and *peoples*. Storytelling then becomes a lens through which we can envision our way out of cognitive imperialism, where we can create models and mirrors where none existed, and where we can experience the spaces of freedom and justice.

Storytelling becomes a space where we can escape the gaze and the cage of the Empire, even if it is just for a few minutes.

Oral storytelling becomes an even more important vehicle for the creation of free cognitive spaces because the physical act of gathering a group of people together within our territories reinforces the web of relationships that stitch our communities together. The storyteller then has to work with emergence and flux, developing a unique relationship with the audience based entirely on context and relationships. Whose is in the audience? Where are they from? Which clans are present? What age groups? What challenges are individuals, families and communities going through? What personal gifts does the audience bring with them? What emotions do people bring? Which moon are we in? This context provides the storyteller with information s/he uses to decide what to tell and how to tell it to gain both individual meaning and collective resonance. The relationship between those present becomes dynamic, with the storyteller adjusting their "performance"[46] based on the reactions and presence of the audience. The lines between storyteller and audience become blurred as individuals make non-verbal (and sometimes verbal) contributions to the collective event. The "performance," whether a song, a dance or a spoken word story, becomes then an individual and collective experience, with the goal of lifting the burden of colonialism by visioning new realities.

While this is now also accomplished by Indigenous artists through the written word, spoken word, theatre, performance art, visual art, music and rap, film and video, it is most powerful in terms of transformation in its original cultural context because that context places dynamic relationships at the core. When mediated through print or recording devices, these relationships become either reduced (technology that limits interactivity) or unilateral (as in print, film, or video, when the creator cannot respond to the reaction of the audience). Then the process, to me, loses some of its transformative power because it is no longer emergent.

Storytelling is an important process for visioning, imagining, critiquing the social space around us, and ultimately challenging the colonial norms fraught in our daily lives. In a similar way, dreams and visions propel resurgence because they provide Nishnaabeg with both the knowledge from the spiritual world and processes for real-izing those visions. Dreams and visions provide glimpses of decolo-nized spaces and transformed realities that we have collectively yet to imagine.

This is a thread that runs through this entire book, but begins here with the consideration of a Creation Story. There are several differ-ent Creation Stories within Nishnaabeg cosmology and these stories are epics in and of themselves, often taking several hours or even days to tell. It is not ethically appropriate for me to tell these stories here, since these stories are traditionally told by Elders who carry these re-sponsibilities during ceremony or under certain circumstances. They are not widely shared. However, sketches of these stories have been printed by some of those Elders themselves.[47] Relying on these pub-lished version and versions I have heard told in workshops and Elders Conferences (so in public *not* ceremonial contexts), I wish to bring at-tention to four tenets of the story that directly relate to the role of in-tellectual pursuits and theory in relation to resurgence; and I want to reclaim the context for interpretation of these teachings. One print version of this story is by Eddie Benton-Banai and is known as the Seven Fires of Ojibway Creation.[48] The following version was told to me by Edna Manitowabi, and she spent a lot of time explaining this story in the context of her own life and in the context of her work with our young women. It is printed here with her permission.

Grandmother Teachings[49]
Edna Manitowabi

My name is Asinykwe and I am a relative of Mkwa, the Bear. I am from Wiikwemikong, Mnidoo Minising. My father was Gaazongii (John Mnidoo Abi). My mother was Naakwegiizigokwe,[50] (Mary Louise Trudeau) and she was a relative of Jijak (Crane). My mother lost nine children to residential school. I was the last to go. I went searching for these teachings as a way of recovering from this loss.

Dreamtime has always been a great teacher for me. I see my dreams as guides or mentors, as the Grandfathers and Grandmothers giving me direction in my life. Dreams are how my own spirit guides me through my life. In the mid 1970s, a dream led me to ceremonies and to the Little Boy water drum. When I first heard the sound of the Little Boy and felt his incredible vibration quivering through every cell and every fiber of my being, I knew I had come home, because I had dreamed of that Little Boy long before then.

I vividly recall the way the Little Boy was dressed the first time I saw him. He wore a headband with Seven Teaching Stones on his head. These symbolize the Seven Fires or the Seven Stages. I have tried to live my life according to these teachings, especially now as I move into my senior years. The time has come for me as a Grandmother, a teacher and a Great Grandmother to pass these on to the next generation of women. I have taken up this work and these responsibilities and now I must remember these teachings, wear them, and pass them on to the younger generation of women who are now coming into that power time as a new woman spirit.

For a number of years now, I have had the honour and the privilege of preparing our young girls as they move into womanhood, and for helping young women, Mothers and Aunties who want to change their lives and have new understandings as Oshki-Nishnaabekwe[51] and as Ogichitaa.[52] These are not easy transitions to make. As a Grandmother, I try to help young women understand what is happening to them when their Grandmother comes to visit for the first time.[53] It is important that we as Grandmothers, Mothers, and Aunties come together as women to help and support these young women. This is particularly important now as our Mother the Earth is going through her own cleansing. We reflect this cleansing when we renew ourselves with these teachings, ceremonies, fasting and our rites of passage. We need to pass on the teachings of the sacredness of the water that sustains us, the air that we breathe, and the fire within us, so that our next generation of women have an understanding of what is happening to them during this powerful transition. Through these teachings they will then come to understand the Earth as their Mother. Through these teachings, they will then come to understand the Earth as themselves.

They will understand her seasons, her moods and her cycles.
They will understand that she is the Mother to all of Creation.

They will understand that she takes care of herself.

They will see that she is beautiful, sacred and that she was created first.

They will know that she holds a special place in our hearts because she is our Mother.

They will understand that our people connect to this land as their Mother.

We need to help our young people maintain this relationship and these teachings, because that connection is the umbilical bond to all of Creation.

When our young women understand this, they will understand their own seasons, cycles and moods. They will understand that they are sacred and beautiful. They will understand that they must take care of themselves, and that they are the mothers to generations yet to be born.

We do this for our young women so they will be guided by our Mother's wisdom and so they will model themselves after this Earth. So they might grow up to be good and kind compassionate Anishinaabekwewag. So they might know how to look after their children and their grandchildren. So that together, we might be a strong nation again. That is my dream. That is why I keep working. We do this work because we love our children. This is my purpose in life as a Grandmother and a Great Grandmother. This is my purpose in life as a Kobaade.[54]

In the beginning, before the beginning, there was only darkness and emptiness. In this cold, dark, vastness there was a sound, a sound like the shaking of seeds in a gourd. Then there was one thought, the first thought. The thought of the Great Mystery, Creator, Gzhwe Mnidoo.[55]

Gzhwe Mnidoo's thoughts went out into the darkness. S/he knew s/he had to create a place for these thoughts, so Gzhwe Mnidoo created a circle in that darkness and within that circle s/he made a fire. At the centre of the circle was the heart beat of the Creator.

In the beginning, the first thought was the pulse and rhythm of Gzhwe Mnidoo. The thoughts and the heartbeat went out into the vastness. The thoughts and the vibrational sound of the heartbeat created the star world, the sky, and the universe. The Creator's first thought combined with the first heartbeat became the First Fire of Creation.

Within that great circle of the universe came another circle when Gzhwe Mnidoo made a fire creating light in that darkness. This is Creator's Second Fire, Giizis, the Sun. Within that great circle was the partner to the Giizis, our Grandmother the Moon. Dibiki-Giizis is the nighttime sun who would give us light in our darkness— the duality of all was created.

Grandmother Moon is the Grand woman of the universe and was given to us to govern the cycles. The seasons would renew all the life that would be created. The partnership of night and day was established and this was the Third Fire of Creation. All of this was set into motion with the four sacred directions, and in doing so movement was created, the Fourth Fire of Creation.

Gzhwe Mnidoo then called on the beneshiinyak[56] of every colour, song, size and shape. Gzhwe Mnidoo put all of the thoughts and creative energy into seeds and asked the beneshiinyak to spread the seeds. Those seeds carried all of the creative energy, all of the thoughts and the potential for all of life. This was the Fifth Fire of Creation.

Then Gzhwe Mnidoo made a place for those seeds to go. S/he made the most beautiful Woman, who we know as our Mother the Earth. Three times, Gzhwe Mnidoo tried. On the fourth try, s/he made our beautiful, round earth. Gzhwe Mnidoo gave her a heart from the First Fire and placed it at the very core of her being. The very first woman created was a woman with a heart, with emotion, and it was a woman with a heart that would give birth to all of Creation.

Gzhwe Mnidoo looked upon Creation, the incredible beauty of the Earth, the waterways, the lakes and streams, the rivers. Her Life Blood flowing below and above the ground. These are the very waters of life that feed and nourish all of life, all of Creation. Her veins and her lifeblood, her bloodlines give life to all that Gzhwe Mnidoo had made. In all of that we would always know that we are joined together as one. We have the same Mother. We would always know she was created first, the first woman with a heart. When Creator finished Creation, Gzhwe Mnidoo gave it to her. You are the Creator now, you will create life and renew it. This is why these teachings are so important to our young women — when we bring forth new life we are reenacting this story.

When the seeds had been scattered on the face of the Earth, Gzhwe Mnidoo saw the beauty of her and how everything moved in harmony and in balance. Gzhwe Mnidoo saw how everything was full and so complete and Creator was filled with great joy. Gzhwe Mnidoo was filled with tears at this great joy, and they fell to the earth nourishing the land and the seeds mated to the soil.

And so from her breast, from her, came all that there is, and all that there will be; the winged of the air, the swimmers, the four legged, the flowers, the plants, the crawlers, the trees, and the seas that moved across the land. Upon her bosom reigned peace and happiness for ages and ages, and this was the Sixth Fire of Creation.

Original Man was the last to be created. Gzhwe Mnidoo wanted one who would reflect her/his thoughts, and so from the first woman s/he took four parts of her body — soil, air, water and fire and molded a being, a vessel. Gzhwe Mnidoo blew his/her own spirit breath into the being and gave him her/his own thoughts, and these thoughts were so vast that they spilled out of his head into his entire body. Gzhwe Mnidoo touched Original Man's breast causing his heart to beat in harmony with the rhythm of the universe and with Gzhwe Mnidoo.

Gzhwe Mnidoo then lowered him down to the Earth so that he might also be a child of the great Mother. It is in that and with great kindness and humility, with the utmost gentleness, that Anishinaabe touched and met his Mother. This is the Seventh Fire of Creation.

This story is important for young women to know because they re-create this story in pregnancy. When we create new life, it is an extension of ourselves, just as Original Man was an extension of Gzhwe Mnidoo. In the same way, our thoughts, our breath, and our heartbeat, pulses in the new life we carry in our sacred waters.

Our Theory is Personal [57]

A theory in its most basic form is simply an explanation for why we do the things we do. When we think of theory in this way, the Aandisokaanan and our language encodes our theories, and we express those theories in both the Dibaajimowinan[58] and our ways of being in the world. I have come to understand the Dibaajimowinan as echoing the Aandisokaanan. Our personal creation stories—our lives, mirror and reflect the Seven Fires of Creation.

The starting point within Indigenous theoretical frameworks then is different than from within western theories: the spiritual world is alive and influencing; colonialism is contested; and storytelling, or "narrative imagination," is a tool to vision other existences outside of the current ones by critiquing and analyzing the current state of affairs, but also by dreaming and visioning other realities.[59] The responsibility for finding meaning within these Aandisokaanan lies within individual Nishnaabeg; and this is communicated through our Dibaajimowinan. Every Nishnaabeg has our own personal stories or narratives that communicate their personal truths, learning, histories and insights. Dibaajimowinan in this sense are personal opportunities to create. Our Elders consider Creation Stories to be of paramount importance because they provide the ontological and epistemological framework to interpret other Aandisokaanan and Dibaajimowinan in a culturally inherent way. It is critical then, that these stories themselves are interpreted in a culturally inherent way, rather than through the obfuscated lens of imperial thought, because they are foundational and they serve to build meaning into the other stories.

The first insight into Nishnaabeg theoretical foundations I would like to explore occurs in the Seventh Fire of creation, after Gzhwe Mnidoo[60] has dreamed the physical world through the first Six Fires. The First Fire created the universe through the union of the first thought (intellectual knowledge) with the first heartbeat (heart-knowledge or emotion, truth). In the Second Fire, Gzhwe Mnidoo created the first fire and the Four Directions. In the Third Fire duality exists for the first time. The Fourth Fire brings movement. By combining duality and movement, Gzhwe Mnidoo encapsulated his thoughts into seeds (the Fifth Fire), and the Sixth Fire was the creation of the first woman as a mother, the earth so those seeds would have somewhere to go.

Gzhwe Mnidoo next created the first beings, but it took a very, very long time. S/he wanted to create the most beautiful beings possible. So

Gzhwe Mnidoo dreamed. Gzhwe Mnidoo visioned. Gzhwe Mnidoo took time, tried some things out. S/he was careful and persistent, and finally, after a good length of time, Gzhwe Mnidoo lowered the first being, ever so gently to earth. Nishna is our verb for "being lowered." Reclaiming the context of this story means that rather than saying or thinking that Gzhwe Mnidoo lowered an abstract "first person" to the earth, if I am a woman, I say or think Gzhwe Mnidoo lowered "the first woman to the earth."[61]

That first being was the most beautiful thing Gzhwe Mnidoo had every seen, and Gzhwe Mnidoo's heart swelled with love. Again, our Elders teach us that this most beautiful, perfect lovely being was not just any "First Person," but that it was me, or you. We are taught to insert ourselves into the story. Gzhwe Mnidoo created the most beautiful, perfect person possible and that most beautiful, perfect person was me, Betasamosake.[62] What does this tell us about Nishnaabeg thought?

It is personal.

We were created out of love.

That the love of Gzhwe Mnidoo is unconditional, complete, and that s/he loves us the way we are, without judgment.

By inserting ourselves into these stories, we assume responsibilities — responsibilities that are not necessarily bestowed upon us by the collective, but that we take on according to our own gifts, abilities and affiliations. Nishnaabeg theory has to be learned in the context of our own personal lives, in an emotional, physical, spiritual and intellectual way. Every time I tell my children this story, or they hear this part of it in ceremony, their faces light up. It re-affirms that they are good, and beautiful and perfect they way they are. Every time I have shared this part of our creation story with Indigenous students, their faces light up as well. When interpreted this way, our stories draw individuals into the resurgence narrative on their own terms and in accordance to their own names, clan affiliations and gifts. For just a moment, they are complete in the absence of want — decolonizing one moment at a time. Indigenous thought can only be learned through the personal; this is because our greatest influence is on ourselves, and because living in a good way is an incredible disruption of the colonial meta-narrative in and of itself. In a system requiring presence, the only way to learn is to live and demonstrate those teachings through a personal embodiment of mino bimaadiziwin. As Edna said in her Creation Story, we *wear* our teachings.

Embodied Knowledge, Unlimited Intelligence

The next part of the story, after Gzhwe Mnidoo has lowered me to the earth, tells us that Gzhwe Mnidoo put her/his right hand to my forehead and s/he transferred all of Gzhwe Mnidoo's thoughts into me. There were so many, that the thoughts couldn't just stay in my head; they spilled into every part of my being and filled up my whole body. Gzhwe Mnidoo's knowledge was so immense from creating the world that it took all of my being to embody it.[63]

This tells us that in order to access knowledge from a Nishnaabeg perspective, we have to engage our entire bodies: our physical beings, emotional self, our spiritual energy and our intellect. Our methodologies, our lifeways must reflect those components of our being and the integration of those four components into a whole. This gives rise to our "research methodologies," our ways of knowing, our processes for living in the world.[64]

It also tells us that there is no limit on Indigenous intellect. Gzhwe Mnidoo dreamt our world into existence. S/he dreamed us into existence, demonstrating that the process of creation—visioning, making, doing—is the most powerful process in the universe. My Creation Story tells me that collectively we have the intellect and creative power to regenerate our cultures, languages and nations. My Creation Story tells me another world is possible and that I have the tools to vision it and bring it into reality. I can't think of a more powerful narrative.

All of the knowledge that Gzhwe Mnidoo possessed from making every aspect of creation was transferred to us. We can access this vast body of knowledge through our cultures by singing, dancing, fasting, dreaming, visioning, participating in ceremony, apprenticing with Elders, practicing our lifeways and living our knowledge, by watching, listening and reflecting in a good way. Ultimately we access this knowledge through the quality of our relationships, and the personalized contexts we collectively create. The meaning comes from the context and the process, not the content.[65] In another way, Sákéj Youngblood Henderson says the meaning comes from the performance of our culture.[66] Gerald Vizenor says the meaning is in the telling and in the presence, our individual and collective presence—Creation as presence.[67] We are all saying the same thing. The performance of our "theories" and thought is how we collectivize meaning. This is important because our collective truths as a nation and as a culture are continuously generated from those individual truths we carry around inside ourselves. Our collective truths exist in a nest of individual diversity.

A little while later in the story, Original Man—or in my case, Betasmosake—goes searching for answers about both the meaning of life and the meaning of her own existence. She finds that for every question she has, Gzhwe Mnidoo has created a story with the answers. She finds that it is her responsibility to discover those stories and seek out the answers. This is our journey through resurgence. This is our responsibility. We are each responsible for finding our own meanings, for shifting those meanings through time and space, for coming to our own meaningful way of being in the world. We are each responsible for being present in our own lives and engaged in our own realities.

Interpreting Creation Stories within a culturally inherent framework provides several insights into Nishnaabeg thought. First, it is highly personal. All Nishnaabeg people are theorists in the sense that they hold responsibilities to making meaning for their own creation and their own life. This happens in the context of Nishnaabeg Knowledge, their name, their clan, their community, their own personal gifts and attributes and their own life experience. Theory is collectivized through the telling of our stories and the performance of our ceremonies. We begin to teach our children theory immediately, and they begin to teach us theory immediately. In part because they are fresh from the Spiritual world, with a purity of heart and mind that is difficult to find in adults, but also because they tell it like it is, unaware of whether that is considered "appropriate" or not.

In terms of resurgence, our Creation Stories tell us that collectively and intellectually we have access to all of the knowledge we need to untangle ourselves from the near destruction we are draped in, because Gzhwe Mnidoo transferred all of her/his thoughts into our full bodies. It tells us that each of us must live in a good and balanced way—physically, intellectual, emotionally and spiritually—in order to access this knowledge. For me, it took participating in my own Creation Story and the Creation Stories of my children through the ceremonies of pregnancy, birth and mothering that enabled me to understand the deeper meanings of these theories. These ceremonies in my life were profoundly transformative in all aspects of my being, and yet it took seven years to be able to articulate these meanings from within *debwewin*, meaning truth.

---

39 The term "Indigenous theory" or "Indigenous Thought" is problematic because it reinforces an artificial division between thought and embodiment. For Indigenous Peoples, thought is fully integrated into living, being and performance of our traditions. For a more detailed discussion, see Sákéj Youngblood Henderson's *First Nations Jurisprudence and Aboriginal Rights*, Native Law Centre, Saskatoon, SK, 2006). "Indigenous theory" is lived, not just discussed and actualized in the intellectual realm. This will become more apparent in Chapter Five, and I have attempted to use terms from Nishnaabemowin where appropriate.

40 Sákéj Youngblood Henderson, "Postcolonial Ghost Dancing: Diagnosing European Colonialism," in Marie Battiste, ed., *Reclaiming Indigenous Voice and Vision*, UBC Press, Vancouver, 2000, 57–77.

41 I have carefully considered the ethical issues around this discussion and I decided to frame this chapter around published versions (both oral, in the form of public talks and written) of these stories by reputable Nishnaabeg Elders. This means that what is available to widely share is a small fraction of these stories and their meanings. Full understanding only occurs after several years of learning these stories in appropriate oral contexts under the guidance of Elders. I have heard the telling of various versions and parts of this Creation Story over the past fifteen years from a variety of sources including Robin Greene-ba, Edna Manitowabi and Doug Williams. Most recently, Jim Dumont told a similar version to the one I am using for my purposes here at the Elders Conference on February 20, 2010, at Trent University in Peterborough, ON. I have also heard Nishnaabeg educator Nicole Bell retell several aspects of these stories in our local language nest, Wii-Kendimiing Nishnaabemowin Saswaansing. I have relied on these oral versions for the purposes of this book, but they are also similar to Benton-Banai's telling in the *Mishomis Book*.

42 Aandisokaanan are traditional, sacred stories. See Wendy Makoons Geniusz, *Our Knowledge is Not Primitive: Decolonizing Botanical Anishinaabe Teachings*, Syracuse University Press, Syracuse NY, 2009, 12.

43 There are both Four Hill and Seven Hill versions of this concept in Nishnaabeg philosophy.

44 Bell, N., E. Conroy, K. Wheatley, B. Michaud, C. Maracle, J. Pelletier, B. Filion, B. Johnson, "Anishinaabe Creation Story" in The Ways of Knowing Guide, Ways of Knowing Partnership Turtle Island Conservation, Toronto Zoo, Toronto Ontario, 2010, 32, available online at <torontozoo.travel/pdfs/tic/Stewardship_Guide.pdf>. The story present in The Ways of Knowing Guide is based on the Teachings of the Seven Fires of Creation by Edward Benton-Banai, rendered as a poem entitled "The Seven Fires of the Ojibway Nation, originally published in The Sounding Voice, Indian Country Press, 1978, and found in print, page 20 of First Nations Peoples, 2nd Edition by Pamela Williamson and John Roberts, published by Emond Montgomery, Toronto, 2004.

45 Neal McLeod, Cree Narrative Memory: From Treaties to Contemporary Times, Purich Press, Saskatoon SK, 2007, 100.

46 I use this term in the sense of presence and engagement, rather than a performance that is aimed at entertaining the audience.

47 Basil Johnston, Edward Benton-Banai, Doug Williams, Jim Dumont, Edna Manitowabi, Thomas Peacock and Marlene Wisuri have published these tenets in print form, digital form or have discussed these tenets in oral forms in public. Following this lead, I do not discuss our Creation Story further than the boundary they have established.

48 Bell, N., E. Conroy, K. Wheatley, B. Michaud, C. Maracle, J. Pelletier, B. Filion, B. Johnson, "Anishinaabe Creation Story" in The Ways of Knowing Guide, Ways of Knowing Partnership Turtle Island Conservation, Toronto Zoo, Toronto Ontario, 2010, pages 25–32, available online at <torontozoo.travel/pdfs/tic/Stewardship_Guide.pdf>. The story present in The Ways of Knowing Guide is based on the Teachings of the Seven Fires of Creation by Edward Benton-Banai, rendered as a poem entitled "The Seven Fires of the Ojibway Nation, originally published in The Sounding Voice, Indian Country Press, 1978, and found in print, pages 17–20 of First Nations Peoples, 2nd Edition by Pamela Williamson and John Roberts, published by Emond Montgomery, Toronto, 2004.

49 The following section was written by Edna Manitowabi and is printed here with her permission, March 18, 2011, Peterborough, ON.

50 Asinykwe means "Rock Woman." Wiiwemikong refers to Wikwemikong Unceded Indian Reserve. Mnidoo Minising or "Spirit Island" is the Nishnaabeg name for Manitoulin Island, Ontario. Gaazongii means "Grizzly Bear." Naakwegiizigokwe means "Half Day Women."

51 Oshki-Nishnaabekwe means "New Woman."

52 Ogichitaa is a "sacred or holy woman."

53 This is a reference to a visit by Nokomis Giizis, Grandmother Moon, and is a way of talking about a young woman's first menstrual cycle.

54 Kobaade means Great Grandmother and refers to making a link from one generation to another. We are not to keep the teachings, but to pass them on.

55   There is no gender associated with *Gzhwe Mnidoo* and it can be translated as life force, life essence, creator, the great mystery or "that which we do not understand."

56   birds

57   I am using the word *theory* here to mean entities, explanations and engagements that bring about meaning to both the individual and collective.

58   Dibaajimowinan are personal stories, teachings, ordinary stories, narratives and histories. See Wendy Makoons Geniusz, *Our Knowledge is Not Primitive: Decolonizing Botanical Anishinaabe Teachings*, Syracuse University Press, Syracuse NY, 2009, 12. It is my understanding there is not a uniform boundary between the two, or that different Elders and different regions have specific teachings and protocols around which stories are considered sacred and which are personal stories, teachings, ordinary stories, narratives and histories. There is a relationship between the Aandisokaanan and Dibaajimowinan that to me, is like an echo, not a dichotomy.

59   Neal McLeod, *Cree Narrative Memory: From Treaties to Contemporary Times*, Purich Press, Saskatoon SK, 2007, 98.

60   Doug Williams noted that while the terms "God" or "Creator" might invoke feelings of fear, punishment or authority, *Gzhwe Mnidoo* invokes one of awe, warmth, love, total acceptance, and protection. Gzhwe Mnidoo is the one who can see you and accepts you completely. Waawshkigaamagki (Curve Lake First Nation), July 15, 2010.

61   This teaching was reaffirmed to me by Jim Dumont, Elders Conference, Trent University, Peterborough, ON, February 20, 2010; and Edna Manitoba, Guest Lecture INDG 2601, Trent University, September 23, 2010.

62   This teaching was reaffirmed to me by Jim Dumont, Elders Conference, Trent University, Peterborough, ON, February 20, 2010; and Edna Manitoba, Guest Lecture INDG 2601, Trent University, September 23, 2010.

63   This teaching was reaffirmed to me by Jim Dumont, Elders Conference, Trent University, Peterborough, ON, February 20, 2010; and Edna Manitoba, Guest Lecture INDG 2601, Trent University, September 23, 2010.

64   It is my understanding through many conversations with Edna Manitowabi that the story of Original Man and his trip around the earth visiting all aspects of Creation reveals many of our Nishnaabeg ways of knowing. Original Man is our first teacher, or first researcher. Original Man learns about the world by engaging with it. He learns by visiting, observing, reflecting, naming, singing, dancing, listening, learning-by-doing, experimentation, consulting with Elders, story-telling and by engaging in ceremony. For a print version of this story, "Original Man Walks the Earth", see pages 6-12 in Edward Benton-Banai, *The Mishomis Book: The Voice of the Ojibway*, Indian Country Communications, Hayward WI, 1988. Also see Leanne Betasamosake Simpson, "Advancing an Indigenist Agenda: Promoting Indigenous Intellectual Traditions in Research," in Jill Oakes, Rick Riewe, Rachel ten Bruggencate and Ainsly Cogswell, eds., *Sacred Landscapes*, Aboriginal Issues Press, University of Manitoba, Winnipeg, MB, 2009, 141–54.

65 Leanne Betasamosake Simpson, *The Construction of Traditional Ecological Knowledge: Issues, Implications and Insights*, Unpublished PhD Dissertation, University of Manitoba, Winnipeg, MB, 1999.

66 Sákéj Youngblood Henderson, *First Nations Jurisprudence and Aboriginal Rights*, Native Law Centre, Saskatoon, SK, 2006.

67 Gerald Vizenor and Robert Houle, Pine Tree Lecture, Trent University, Peterborough, ON, February 23, 2010; and Gerald Vizenor, *Fugitive Poses: Native American Indian Scenes of Absence and Presence*, University of Nebraska Press, Lincoln, NB, 1998.

Chapter Three

GDI-NWENINAA:[68] OUR SOUND, OUR VOICE

Indigenous languages carry rich meanings, theory and philosophies within their structures. Our languages house our teachings and bring the practice of those teachings to life in our daily existence. The process of speaking Nishnaabemowin, then, inherently communicates certain values and philosophies that are important to Nishnaabeg being. Breaking down words into the "little words" they are composed of often reveals a deeper conceptual—yet widely held—meaning. This part of the language and language learning holds a wealth of knowledge and inspiration in terms of Aanji Maajitaawin. That is because this "learning through the language" provides those who are not fluent with a window through which to experience the complexities and depth of our culture. The purpose of this chapter is to use this approach to deepen our understandings of decolonization, assimilation, resistance and resurgence from within Nishnaabeg perspectives.

Biskaabiiyang

Biskaabiiyang is a verb that means to look back.[69] The Seventh Generation Institute, located in the northwestern part of Anishinabek territory, has been working with several Elders to develop an Anishinabek process for their MA program in Indigenous thought. They call the first part of their process Biskaabiiyang. In this context it means "returning to ourselves," a process by which Anishinabek researchers and scholars can evaluate how they have been impacted by colonialism in all realms of being.[70] Conceptually, they are using Biskaabiiyang in the same way Indigenous scholars have been using the term "decolonizing"—

to pick up the things we were forced to leave behind, whether they are songs, dances, values, or philosophies, and bring them into existence in the future. Wendy Makoons Geniusz, an Anishinaabe scholar from Wisconsin, uses this approach in her PhD dissertation research and explains:

> Biskaabiiyang research is a process through which Anishinaabe researchers evaluate how they personally have been affected by colonization, rid themselves of the emotional and psychological baggage they carry from this process, and then return to their ancestral traditions ... When using Biskaabiiyang methodologies, an individual must recognize and deal with this negative kind of thinking before conducting research. This is the only way to conduct new research that will be beneficial to the continuation of anishnaabe-gikendaasowin (knowledge, information, and the synthesis of personal teachings) and anishnaabeg-izhitwaawin (anishnaabe culture, teachings, customs, history).
>
> The foundations of Biskaabiiyang approaches to research are derived from the principles of *anishnaabe-inaadiwiwin* (anishnaabe psychology and way of being). These principles are *gaa-izhi-zhawendaagoziyang*: that which was giving to us in a loving way (by the spirits). They have developed over generations and have resulted in a wealth of *aadizookaan* (traditional legends, ceremonies); *dibaajimowin* (teachings, ordinary stories, personal stories, histories) and *anishnaabe izhitwaawin* (anishnaabe culture, teachings, customs, history). Through Biskaabiiyang methodology, this research goes back to the principles of anishnaabe-inaadiziwin in order to decolonize or reclaim anishnaabe-gikendaasowin.[71]

The power of Biskaabiiyang as a process is that once engaged in this process, it becomes obvious and necessary to think of Biskaabiiyang not just in relation to research, but also in relation to how we live our lives as Nishnaabeg people. In our current occupied state, it becomes important to carry the essence of Biskaabiiyang with me through my daily life; it is not something that I can do at the beginning of a project and then forget. We are still enmeshed in the insidious nature of colonialism and neo-colonialism, and this means that I need to keep Biskaabiiyang present in my mind when I am making my way through the world. Biskaabiiyang is a process by which we can figure out how to live as Nishnaabeg in the contemporary world and use our gaa-izhi-zhawendaagoziyang to build a Nishnaabeg renaissance.

Biskaabiiyang has to be an ongoing individual process. However, we cannot effectively engage in Biskaabiiyang in an isolated fashion. As communities of people, we need to support each other in this process and work together to stitch our cultures and lifeways back together. In this way, Biskaabiiyang is both an individual and collective process that we must continually replicate. This is why the larger critical Indigenous intellectual community is important. The contestation of imperial domination becomes our collective and individual starting point, and the lens through which to view our own liberation. As demonstrated in the coming chapters, the personal is always embedded intrinsically into our thought ways and theories; and it is always broadly interpreted within the nest of the collective.

Within Nishnaabeg theoretical foundations, Biskaabiiyang does not literally mean returning to the past, but rather re-creating the cultural and political flourishment of the past to support the well-being of our contemporary citizens. It means reclaiming the fluidity around our traditions, not the rigidity of colonialism; it means encouraging the self-determination of individuals within our national and community-based contexts; and it means re-creating an artistic and intellectual renaissance within a larger political and cultural resurgence. When I asked my Michi Saagiig Nishnaabeg Elder Gdigaa Migizi about Biskaabiiyang, the term immediately resonated with him when English terms such as "resistance" and "resurgence" did not. He explained Biskaabiiyang in terms of a "new emergence,"[72] noting that he lives his own interpretations of the teachings he received from his Elders, just as my generation has the responsibility of finding meaning in the teachings our Elders share with us.

I first encountered the concept of Biskaabiiyang in Wendy Makoons Geniusz's *Our Knowledge Is Not Primitive: Decolonizing Botanical Anishinaabe Teachings*. The concept resonated with me; but because she is from the northwest part of our territory and I do not know her personally, I took the concept first to my language teacher and then to my Elder. I did this because I have learned that unless concepts have local meaning, it is difficult for them to have local resonance. I also thought that as a Michi Saagiig Nishnaabeg person, I could only really learn to understand this concept from within the web of relationships of my existence. While Biskaabiiyang might be an important and powerful cultural way to ground decolonization and resurgence work in other places, it was only going to be useful to me if it had meaning within my current relationships. Both my language teacher and my Elder immediately recognized the word and identified with the concept, which is not always the case when I bring them writing and words from Nishnaabeg writers. Biskaabiiyang then became a very useful and important Nishnaabeg way of grounding resurgence or decolonization as a "new emergence," because it carries wide meaning and has resonance throughout our territory. To me, Biskaabiiyang means not just an evisceration of colonial thinking within individuals before a research project begins; it is a constant continual evaluation of colonialism within both individuals and communities. It also encompasses a visioning process where we create new and just realities in which our ways of being can flourish. Nonetheless, it is not just a visioning process. We must act to create those spaces—be they cognitive or spatial, temporal or spiritual—even if those spaces only exist for fragments of time.

While Biskaabiiyang encompasses the process for decolonizing, the term *Zhaaganashiiyaadizi* encompasses the process and description of living as a colonized or assimilated person.[73] Zhaaganashiiyaadizi occurs when a person tries to live his or her life as a non-Native at the expense of being Nishnaabeg. In other words, they become assimilated. Zhaaganashiiyaadizi is a process by which choices are made to the detriment of being Nishnaabeg. The key is "at the expense of being Nishnaabeg," so one may adopt the ways of the non-Natives only to the extent that it does not negatively influence the core of one's being.[74] I would caution against a racialized understanding of this term. My understanding of this word is indicative of the processes or the continual decisions that one might chose to make—decisions and choices which, in this case, supplant all of the beautiful and diverse ways of living as an contemporary Nishnaabeg. To me this means that we do not need to "go back" to "hunting with bows and arrows," but we do need to practice ways of being and living in the world that are profoundly Nishnaabeg. It also means that there is a diversity of ways of being within a Nishnaabeg value system that encompasses being Nishnaabeg. For me, that means that there isn't a single way of being Nishnaabeg. Rather, there is a set of processes, values, and philosophies embedded in our language and culture that one needs to embrace in order to live as Nishnaabeg. When viewed through a cultural lens, Biskaabiiyang is far from promoting an essential Nishnaabeg identity; instead, it promotes a diversity of political and cultural viewpoints within the Nishnaabeg worldview. There are many good ways to be Nishnaabe, but those ways are constructed and exist within our knowledge and our language.

However, to be able to appreciate that fluidity and diversity, one needs an in-depth knowledge of culture, language, philosophies and anishnaabe-gikendaasowin.

When we speak broadly about Indigenous resistance, we are essentially speaking about processes we engage in to prevent Zhaaganashiiyaadizi (our people from becoming colonized or assimilated). To me, that means we need to act against political processes that undermine our traditional forms of governance, our political cultures, our intellectual traditions, the occupation and destruction of our lands, violence against our children and women, and a host of many other issues. We must learn Nishnaabeg Gikendaasowin and Nishnaabemowin.

While Biskaabiiyang is a useful context to begin to explore what liberation and resurgence looks like within Indigenous thought, it is just the beginning. For Nishnaabeg people, our political and social cultures were profoundly non-hierarchical, non-authoritarian and non-coercive.[75] Our culture placed a profound importance on individuals figuring out their own path, or their own theoretical understanding of their life and their life's work based on individual interpretation of our philosophies, teachings, stories and values. In combination with their own interpretation of the name or names they held within their society, clan responsibilities, and personal gifts or attributes, individuals were afforded a high level of autonomy within the community for exploring and expressing their responsibilities. This is sometimes framed as an "ethic of non-interference"[76] on the part of other community members. It is also coupled or twinned with individual responsibilities of figuring out one's place in the cosmos and how to contribute to the collective while respecting oneself and one's inner being.

Aanjigone

In exploring this "ethic of non-interference" with Elder Gdigaa Migizi, the Nishnaabe concept of Aanjigone emerged. Aanjigone is the idea that one needs to be very, very careful with making judgments and with the act of criticism. Aanjigone is a concept that promotes the framing of Nishnaabeg values and ethics in the positive. It means that if we criticize something, our spiritual being may take on the very things we are criticizing. It promotes non-interference by bringing forth the idea that if someone else does wrong, the "implicate order"[77] will come back on that person and correct the imbalance in some other way. Take an example from Gdigaa Migizi: if we "destroy the land to build a monster cottage on the side of a lake, we can expect this to come back on us in a negative way."[78] There is then no need to criticize or be angry with the perpetrators because they will pay the price for their destructive action, one way or another, and this will be mediated by the Spiritual world. Our responsibility is to live our lives according to the teachings and values that were given to us with great love by Gzhwe Mnidoo.[79] But where does Aanjigone leave us in terms of building resurgence and protecting our lands? And what does Aanjigone mean in terms of the interrogation of colonialism? Academic critique?

Aanjigone ensures that if change or transformation occurs, it promotes Nishnaabeg ways of being and prevents Zhaaganashiiyaadizi. It also ensures that the interrogation or critique of decisions—or the consideration of all the possible consequences of a particular decision—is focused on the concept or decision rather than an individual. In a sense, critique is an internal process and the outcome is an individual action rather than an attack on another. Indeed, when an Elder is displeased with an action of one of his or her students, the Elder does not criticize that action, but is silent. Often at a later point, the Elder will use a story or an activity to convey a particular teaching in an indirect manner.

Very early on in my academic career as a PhD student, a non-Aboriginal academic began attacking my work and the work of my colleagues, writing that we had invented Indigenous Knowledge to propel our own careers, and that no such intellectual capabilities exists within Indigenous Peoples. The paper was immediately accepted for publication. My immediate reaction was to write a scathing academic critique of this particular paper. I consulted Anishinaabeg Elder Robin Greene-ba and asked for his thoughts. I particularly wanted to know if it was ethical for me as a Nishnaabekwe to intellectually attack the paper and critique this scholarship. There was no doubt in my mind that this was the correct thing to do as an academic. Robin answered my question by telling me a story. What I understood from his story was that the better way to proceed was to write a paper about what I thought Indigenous Knowledge was, about why it is important, and about how to promote it in a good way. He made sure I understood that I had a responsibility to do something. But he told me that particular story so I understood that what was truly important was *how* I took on that responsibility.

To me, this means that we must not spend all of our time interrogating and criticizing. We need to spend an enormous amount of energy recovering and rebuilding at this point. Critique and revelation cannot in and of themselves create the kinds of magnificent change our people are looking for. We can only bring about that change by engaging in Biskaabiiyang. To me it means we need to be careful with our criticism. We should not blindly follow the academy's love affair with criticism, ripping apart other Indigenous academics' work—with whom we probably have more in common than virtually any other academics in the world. Instead, we should highlight the positive within each other's work, and save our criticism for the forces that continually try to rip us apart. As Nishnaabeg legal scholar John Borrows writes, "[what Treuer views as authentic and inauthentic voices in Native American writing] … I view [as] different styles and methods of writing within Anishinabek genres and traditions. Recognizing diversity within Anishinabek expression allows for variations between authors, including the use of mixed metaphors, misplaced dialects, fragmentary memories, and fluid identities."[80]

Aanjigone, as I understand it, means to focus within. Although I believe that part of Biskaabiiyang requires criticism and critical thinking, I think Aanjigone propels me towards the idea of focusing the majority of my energy on Nishnaabeg flourishment. Focusing within, I believe Nishnaabeg philosophies are telling me to live my life using Biskaabiiyang and Aanjigone to the best of my gifts and abilities. My interpretation of Aanjigone does not exclude taking action against the colonizer to protect our lands, our knowledge or our lives. Rather, it encourages us to think carefully and strategically about our responses rather than blindly reacting out of anger.

Naakgonige

The third concept I want to discuss by way of introduction into Nishnaabeg resurgence is Naakgonige.[81] Naakgonige is a culturally embedded concept that means to carefully deliberate and decide when faced with any kind of change or decision. It warns against changing for the sake of change, and reminds Nishnaabeg that our Elders and our Ancestors did things a certain way for a reason. For instance, Nishnaabeg did not (and do not) tell traditional Aandisokaanan stories in the spring, summer and fall. When I asked Gdigaa Migizi why, he explained that the spirits were farther away from the earth in winter and less likely to be offended. But he also said that it was his understanding that "something had happened" or an Elder "saw something" that caused them to conduct themselves in a certain way to avoid danger. He explained that we need to trust our Ancestors on certain things. When I asked him how he felt about contemporary storytellers and writers ignoring the tradition of only telling certain stories in the winter, he avoided passing judgment. He told me that he has no idea what they might have done beforehand to ensure that it was a good thing to do. Perhaps they had prayed and asked the spirits for guidance and that led them to make the decision. He only knew that he would not tell certain stories unless there was snow on the ground. In a similar way, Edna Manitowabi explained to me that we do not tell Animal stories or Nanabush stories in the spring, summer and fall because these beings are awake and active during this time and they could be around when we are speaking about them. While she was speaking, I thought about how my children react when I tell stories about them while they are present. They are often embarrassed, even if the stories are delightful in nature. In fact, most adults would feel the same. It makes complete sense that Nishnaabeg would offer the same level of respect to animals and spiritual entities.[82] It also ensures that we take our time with the winter stories and allow ourselves plenty of time to think about them. Similarly, Nishnaabemowin language expert Shirley Williams explained to me that the word *Aandisokaanan* also means that one is calling the spirits you are talking about,[83] something that should be done according to protocol and tradition. Naakgonige encourages one to deliberate and consider the impacts of decisions on all aspects of life and our relationships—the land, the clans, children, and the future. In a sense, it protected our people from engaging in Zhaaganashiiyaadizi because the process of Naakgonige meant that change, even on a personal level, was a long and deliberate process.

Naakgonige encourages Nishnaabeg people to make decisions slowly and carefully. Other words in Nishnaabemowin have meanings that are related to Naakgonige, warning to be careful or mindful. However, Naakgonige has a larger conceptual meaning. Another related word is *Naanaagede'enmowin*, the art of thinking to come to a decision. This is similar to Naakgonige in that it asks a person to sit and reflect on the weighing or measurement of a problem in order to figure out what needs to be done. It is a sorting of one's thoughts so that a decision can be made, a plan to help out the caring part of the individual to listen and care for the heart and do the right thing. The heart must help or guide the mind to come to a good decision.[84]

To me, both the concepts of Naakgonige and Naanaagede'enmowin exemplify resistance. First, because they protect against Zhaaganashiiyaadizi. Second, they are culturally embedded processes that require individuals, clans and communities to carefully deliberate, not just in an intellectual sense, but using their emotional, physical and spiritual beings as well. For instance, if a language speaker were to engage in Naakgonige and Naanaagede'enmowin to decide whether or not to speak Nishnaabemowin to their children, they would have to consider the impact of that act on the child's ability to perform their cultural responsibilities to their family, clan, community and nation. They would have to consider how that choice would impact the values of the child and their relationship to their territory. They would have to assess how that child would interact with Elders and the spiritual aspects of Nishnaabeg culture. They would have to consider the impact on that child's identity, and their ability to comprehend what it is to be Nishnaabeg. The speaker would have to consider not only that child, but also the subsequent generations of the family; and they would have to allow their heart, or their emotional intellect, to guide that decision. By engaging Naakgonige and Naanaagede'enmowin, far fewer people might choose to speak only English to their children; or at the very least, more people may try to mitigate some of the negative impacts that loss of language might have on their family. Rather than blindly accepting the colonizers' truths or acting out of fear, Naakgonige and Naanaagede'enmowin demand presence of mind and heart, engagement, thorough analysis, and a critical evaluation of the long-term impacts of decision making in terms of promoting mino bimaadiziwin and preventing Zhaaganashiiyaadizi—which, in my mind, is what resistance is all about.

I have thought a lot about how my Ancestors lived in the world. And over the past two decades, the values that have always stood out to me or that have been demonstrated to me, particularly through Elders, has been one of profound gentleness and profound kindness. In an interview with the Office of Specific Claims & Research in 1976, Nishnaabeg Elder Peter O'Chiese relayed that one of the first things given to the Nishnaabeg by Gzhwe Mnidoo was to be kind and have a gentle heart.[85] This idea permeates our culture and is expressed through countless words, stories and teachings. The word "Nengaajdoodimoowin—the art of being gentle or of doing something gentle to someone,"[86] is one expression of this idea. Gentleness was seen as strength because gentle people are highly sensitive to potential threats against mino bimaadiziwin. They are highly in tune with peace, the proper use of power and heart knowledge. It is that heart knowledge I would like to consider next.

Debwewin

Nishnaabeg Elder Jim Dumont explained the origins of the word *debwewin* to a group of students and community members at Trent University's Annual Elders Conference in 2010. The word is normally translated as truth, and Dumont explained to us that he had difficulty breaking it down into its components, until an Elder told him to place the letter "o" in front of it. When one does that, the first component of the word is "ode" which means heart. The component "we" means the sound of. So (o)debwewin is "the sound of the heart;" or more specifically, in my own case, it is the sound of my heart. This means my truth will be different from someone else's.[87] This idea has also been described by Murray Sinclair as a plurality of truth.[88] Elder Peter O'Chiese explained that each of the seven original clans has their own truth; and when you put those together, a new or eighth truth emerges.[89] These understandings are philosophically similar to Basil Johnston's explanation:

> Our word for truth or correctness or any of its synonyms is *w'dae'b'wae*, meaning 'he or she is telling the truth, is right, is correct, is accurate.' From its composition—the prefix *dae*, which means 'as far as, inasmuch as, according to,' and the root *wae*, a contraction of *wae-wae*, referring to sound—emerges the second meaning, which gives the sense of a person casting his or her knowledge as far as he or she can. By implication, the person whom is said to be *dae'b'wae* is acknowledged to be telling what he or she knows only insofar as he or she has perceived what he or she is reporting, and only according to his or her command of the language. In other words, the speaker is exercising the highest degree of accuracy possible given what he or she knows. In the third sense, the term conveys the philosophic notion that there is no such thing as absolute truth.[90]

These explanations are consistent with John Borrows' explanation of diversity in terms of Nishnaabeg thought. Borrows explains that difference exists within Nishnaabeg thought. Rather than positioning this difference as "tension" or in an oppositional framing, diversity and difference are seen as necessary parts of the larger whole. The views expressed in this book are my own interpretations as a Nishnaabekwe from the gdigaa bzhiw doodem (bobcat clan) of the Michi Saagiig

Nishnaabeg territory, as a mother, as an intellectual and a language learner. For me, gender plays an important role in my own perspectives, but my understandings of gender are not fully shared by other members of my nation. I have been taught that in the past, gender was conceptualized differently than the binary between male and female expressed in colonial society.[91] For Nishnaabeg people there was fluidity around gender in terms of roles and responsibilities. Often one's name, clan affiliation, ability and individual self-determination positioned one in society more than gender, or perhaps in addition to gender. While I am not comfortable being confined to an essentialized version of Native womanhood defined by child birth,[92] I am also someone who has been profoundly transformed through giving birth, nursing and mothering. I will not apologize for fully participating in those ceremonies and honouring the teachings given to me through those ceremonies.

Andrea Smith reminds us that a critical interrogation of heteropatriarchy must be at the core of nation building, sovereignty and social change.[93] I would argue that this requires a decolonization of our conceptualization of gender as a starting point. Nishnaabeg thought compels us to place the sovereignty of Indigenous women at the core of our movement; but it also compels us to critically evaluate how we are contributing to raising our boys as agents of patriarchy, instead of agents of Biskaabiiyang.

In my own life, I recently used Biskaabiiyang, Naakgonige, Aanjigone and Debwewin to decide whether or not I would wear a long skirt to a sunrise ceremony that took place in my territory. This is an issue full of tension in my territory and I am guessing perhaps in other Nishnaabeg territories as well. In the reclamation of this ceremony, women are generally asked to wear long skirts as a way of showing respect to both our traditions and the conductor as acknowledging our innate power as women and life givers. I have always felt conflicted about this issue. At times I have worn my skirt to demonstrate respect to the Elders and knowledge of those teachings. When I was pregnant and nursing my children, I wanted to be the in skirt to honour those processes. But I have never believed that my value as a woman was tied to my ability to reproduce; and there have been many times when the idea that I was *required* to wear a skirt frustrated and angered me. So a few months ago, when I decided to go to the sunrise ceremony, I decided to listen to the part of me that was profoundly irritated with the required attire.

I first spoke to one of my Grandmother Elders. She explained the teaching, but also said that no one should be forced to wear something or do something they are uncomfortable doing. I put semaa (tobacco) down. I prayed. Then I thought about why I felt so irritated about the skirt in the first place. I thought about how in colonial society, the skirt carries meaning that maintains the rigid boundaries in a two-gendered system. My understanding of gender within my own culture is one that was much more fluid. I thought of my Ancestors and how they might feel watching me at the ceremony in pants. I thought of a photo that hangs in my parents' house of my great great Grandmother, on her trap line in pants. I thought of the some of Nishnaabekwe my own age— how we roll our eyes at the skirt rule—and I tried to think of a more ethical response. I thought of how my being would appear to the spirits if I wore the skirt but resented it. I thought of Gzhwe Mnidoo, the one that loves me in total acceptance and understanding, in warmth, in protection. I thought that Gzhwe Mnidoo cared about who I was, not what I was wearing. I thought about the coming generations. I thought about my four-year-old daughter Minowewebeneshiihn, and then I made my decision.

Gdi-nweninaa

Listening to the sound of our voice means that we need to listen with our full bodies—our hearts, our minds and our physicality. It requires a full presence of being. It requires an understanding of the culturally embedded concepts and teachings that bring meaning to our practices and illuminate our lifeways. In regenerating our languages, an enormous task in and of itself, we must also ask our Elders and fluent speakers to teach us through the language, using specific words as windows into a deeper, layered understanding. We must listen and take with us those sounds that hold the greatest meaning in our own lives and in our resurgence.

68   I would like to acknowledge that the title of this chapter came from a language book of the same name written by Shirley Ida Williams, *Gdi-nweninaa: Our Sound, Our Voice*, Neganigwane Company, Peterborough, ON, 2002. In this chapter, I explore four interrelated Nishnaabeg concepts that provide a window through which people who do not speak Nishnaabemowin (and I am a language learner, not yet a speaker) can begin to understand how concepts of decolonization, resistance, resurgence and truth are expressed within Nishnaabeg existence. While these concepts were not chosen randomly, they are not the only windows into these ideas within the language; there are many, many others.

69   Explained to me by my language tutor Vera Bell, Peterborough, ON, June 19, 2010.

70   Wendy Makoons Geniusz, *Our Knowledge is Not Primitive: Decolonizing Botanical Anishinaabeg Teachings*, Syracuse University Press, Syracuse, NY, 2009, 9.

71   Wendy Makoons Geniusz, *Our Knowledge is Not Primitive: Decolonizing Botanical Anishinaabe Teachings*, Syracuse University Press, Syracuse, NY, 2009, 9–10.

72   Doug Williams, Waawshkigaamagki (Curve Lake First Nation), July 15, 2010.

73   Wendy Makoons Geniusz, *Our Knowledge is Not Primitive: Decolonizing Botanical Anishinaabe Teachings*, Syracuse University Press, Syracuse, NY, 2009, 159, 196. This term was also familiar to Doug Williams, Waawshkigaamagki (Curve Lake First Nation), July 15, 2010.

74   White person

75   I've read about this in Kiera Ladner, "Women and Blackfoot Nationalism," *Journal of Canadian Studies*, 2000, 35(2): 35–61; and it has been demonstrated to me through example by several Elders including Doug Williams Waawshkigaamagki (Curve Lake First Nation) and Robin Greene-ba (Iskatewizaagegan).

76   As described by Rupert Ross, *Dancing with a Ghost: Exploring Indian Reality*, Reed Books Canada, Markham, ON, 1992, 11–38.

77   I am borrowing the term "implicate order" to refer to the spiritual world, from Sákéj Youngblood Henderson, *First Nations Jurisprudence and Aboriginal Rights*, Native Law Centre, University of Saskatchewan, Saskatoon, SK, 2006, 144–153.

78   Doug Williams, Waawshkigaamagki (Curve Lake First Nation), July 15, 2010. Shirley Williams corrected my spelling of this word September 12, 2010.

79   I am using the verb *Gzhwe* rather than *Gchi* or *Kichi* because according to Doug Williams, Gzhwe represents awe, warmth, love, total acceptance, protection and understanding, rather than an authoritarian Creator that is imbued with fear and punishment. Doug Williams explained this to me in Waawshkigaamagki (Curve Lake First Nation), July 15, 2010. Shirley Williams had the same understanding of the word in Peterborough, ON, September 12, 2010.

80   John Borrows, *Drawing Out Law: A Spirit's Guide*, University of Toronto Press, Toronto, ON, 2010, endnote 2, 233; Taiaiake Alfred gives us a real world example

of how differing opinions and dissent was handled in contemporary times within the traditional decision making of his community in "The People," *The Words That Come Before All Else: Environmental Philosophies of the Haudenosaunee*, Haudenosaunee Environmental Task Force, Akwesasne, n.d., 12–13.

81   Naakgonige was explained to me by Elder Doug Williams, Waawshkigaamagki (Curve Lake First Nation), July 15, 2010. Shirley Williams translated this word to mean "to plan" to make plans after deciding what is going to be done, a decision to follow what was said, a plan, a law or a rule.

82   Edna Manitowabi, Stoney Lake, ON, December 13, 2010.

83   Shirley Williams, Peterborough, ON, September 13, 2010.

84   Explained to me by Shirley Williams, Peterborough, ON, September 19, 2010.

85   Peter O'Chiese interview, translated by Harold Cardinal, Office of Specific Claims, Hinton, Alberta, March 1, 1976. Available online at <ourspace.uregina.ca/bitstream/10294/2193/1/IH-198.pdf>. Also see Jim Dumont's "Anishinaabe Izhichigaywin," in *Sacred Water: Water for Life*, Lee Foushee and Renee Gurneau, eds., North American Water Office, Lake Elmo Minnesota, 2010, 13–57.

86   Shirley Williams, Peterborough, ON, September 15, 2010.

87   Jim Dumont, Presentation, Elders Conference, Trent University, Peterborough, ON, February 20, 2010.

88   Murray Sinclair, "Aboriginal Peoples and Euro-Canadians: Two World Views," in John H. Hylton, ed., *Aboriginal Self-Government in Canada: Current Trends and Issues*, Purich Publishing, Saskatoon, SK, 1994, 19.

89   *Final Report of the Royal Commission on Aboriginal Peoples*, Volume 3, Chapter 2, available online at <www.ainc-inac.gc.ca/ch/rcap/sg/sh14_e.htm>.

90   Basil Johnston, *Anishinaubae Thesaurus*, Michigan State University Press, East Lansing, MI, 2007, x.

91   Kiera Ladner, "Women and Blackfoot Nationalism," *Journal of Canadian Studies*, 2000, 35(2): 35–61.

92   Emma LaRoque, "Métis and Feminist" in Joyce Green, ed., *Making Space for Indigenous Feminism*, Fernwood Publishing, Halifax, NS, 2007, 63.

93   Andrea Smith, *Native Americans and the Christian Right*, Duke University Press, Durham, NC, 2008, 255–272.

Chapter Four

NIIMTOOWAAD MIKINAAG GIJIYING BAKONAAN (DANCING ON OUR TURTLE'S BACK): AANDISOKAANAN AND RESURGENCE

Perhaps the most epic narrative in Nishnaabeg thought concerning the processes of mobilization or migration in relation to colonialism, decolonization and resurgence, is communicated through the Seven Fires Prophecy. In a time of peace and flourishment, seven prophets came to the Nishnaabeg people and made seven predictions for the future. The seven prophets also outlined an epic journey from the east coast of Turtle Island to the western shores of the Great Lakes; they encouraged our people to make that journey as a protection against the coming colonizers. The First Fire of the prophecy set in motion the greatest mobilization in Nishnaabeg history: the great migration, in which the nation moved west in waves, taking an estimated five hundred years or ten generations to complete.[94] The migration mitigated the impact of conquest and colonialism on the Nishnaabeg nation by spreading the nation out over a much larger territory, enabling the north and the west some protection from the centres of colonialism in the south and east. As a social movement, the Gete-Nishnaabeg[95] were able to maintain a strategic and organized mass mobilization over an incredibly long period of time. Thinking about the prophecy in this way has made me recognize that we are a culture of mobilization. We are a culture that embodies both movement and collectivity.

What can we learn from the Seven Fires Prophecy about modern-day Nishnaabeg resurgence? To begin, let's focus on the prophecy itself in a little more detail. During the Fourth Fire of the Seven Fires

Prophecy, two prophets came to the people instead of just one. The prophets explained the coming of a light-skinned people who would either come to Nishnaabeg territory with the face of goodwill, or they would come wearing the face of death. The prophets came with many warnings of manipulation and dishonesty, and instructions were given to not trust the light-skinned people until they had proved their good-will. "You will know that the face they wear is the one of death if the rivers run with poison and fish become unfit to eat."[96]

The Fifth and Sixth Fires were periods of immense destruction. European conquest and occupation permeated our territory, yet the prophecy played an important part in the resistance Nishnaabeg people showed during this period. The prophecy of the Seventh Fire foretold of a time when the most oppressive parts of the colonial regime would loosen and Nishnaabeg people would be able to pick up the pieces of their language, culture and thought-ways and begin to build, in essence, a resurgence. So during the Fifth and Sixth Fire, people planned for the Seventh Fire. Scrolls were hidden. Ceremonies were practiced underground with children present. Stories were passed along through the families. Families retreated to the bush whenever possible, as a strategy to avoid Indian Agents, residential schools and child welfare agencies. Some people hung onto the language. Our Grandmothers and Grandfathers planted the seeds of resurgence in the Fifth and Sixth fires. Our responsibilities for resurgence pre-existed before we were present on the earth. In our greatest period of destruction, our Grandparents resisted by planting the seeds of resurgence, just as Gzhwe Mnidoo planted the seeds of life in the Fourth Fire of Creation. For Nishnaabeg thinkers, resistance and resurgence are not only our response to colonialism, they are our only responsibility in the face of colonialism.

Resurgence is our original instruction.

Many Nishnaabeg thinkers believe we are in the period of the Seventh Fire. It is the responsibility of the new people, the Oshkimaadiziig,[97] to pick up the pieces of our lifeways, collectivize them and build a political and cultural renaissance and resurgence. It is also foretold that if this is done in a good way, it has the power to transform settler society generating political relationships based on the

Indigenous principles of peace, justice, and righteousness as embodied in mino bimaadiziwin.

Chibimoodaywin

Three Fires Midewewin leader Eddie Benton-Banai refers to the Seven Fires mobilization as *Chibimoodaywin*.[98] When I asked Nishnaabe Nokomis and Elder Shirley Williams what chibimoodaywin meant, she said, "Not mobilization or migration. It sounds like a long, slow, painful crawl!"[99] This tells us that mobilization, resistance, and resurgence involves sacrifice, persistence, patience and slow, painful movement.

Chibimoodaywin was a social movement that was inspired by a spiritual vision, debated and planned by spiritual leaders, intellectuals and political leadership, and ultimately carried out by our families. Again, our Elders estimate it took five hundred years to complete ten generations of Nishnaabeg people. The commitment, persistence, solidarity, and determination of ten generations carrying out a single vision is outstanding. Debate, respect for dissenting voices, consensus, and the respect for the sovereignty of individuals, families and clans, allowed the spread of Nishnaabeg people as a movement of energy over the land, branching out through the Great Lakes region. Their community procession lasted five hundred years. Imagine what we could accomplish with a committed, strategic persistent resurgence movement over the next ten generations. Chibimoodaywin inspires me to begin to try and reclaim the community-based processes that inspired *generations* of Nishnaabeg people to mobilize and to carry out this prophecy.

Chibimoodaywin tells me that spiritual visioning, followed by individual commitment and action, is a cornerstone of Nishnaabeg mobilization, resistance and now, resurgence. But our ancestors must have also had a fantastic ability to generate mass support for individual visions, and to carry out those visions over long periods of time. To realize and build resurgence we not only need visionaries, but our visionaries must also have the skills to excite, inspire and illuminate our peoples to unite, committing to transform that vision into sustained and committed action.

Re-creation: Niimtoowaad Mikinaag Gijiying Bakonaan[100] (Dancing on Our Turtle's Back)

In the last section of the Seven Fires Prophecy, there is a mirroring of the cycle of creation-destruction-re-creation within Nishnaabeg thought. This cycle sets the stage for interpretation of re-creation as a new emergence or resurgence. This theme is also echoed to current generations through our Re-creation Stories. Within Indigenous thought, there is not a singular vision of resurgence, but many. Elders direct our people to live their lives in a way that promotes positive relationships with the land, their families and all of Creation.[101] This is performed by individuals within the web of the Kokum Dibaajimowinan.[102] These teachings include: Aakde'ewin, the art of having courage; Dbadendiziwin, humility; Debwewin, truth or sincerity; Mnaadendiwin, respect; Nbwaakawin, wisdom; Gwekwaadiziwin, honesty; and Zaagidewin, love (these are discussed in detail in Chapter Seven). Using the theoretical foundations presented in Chapter Two, it means that we all carry responsibilities in terms of resurgence; and that we are also responsible for re-creating the good life in whatever forms we imagine, vision and live in contemporary times. The process of starting over, Aanji Maajitaawin is embodied in our Re-creation Stories.

Waynabozhoo and the Great Flood[103]

This narrative starts with a phase of destruction: the Nishnaabeg had lost their way; they're relationships were imbalanced; and the their lives were permeated with violence and conflict. As a restorative measure, Gzhwe Mnidoo brought a large flood to the lands, not as a punitive act, but as purification designed to re-align the Nishnaabeg with mino bimaadiziwin.

Waynabozhoo managed to save himself by finding a large log floating in the vast expanse of water. In time, more and more animals joined him on the log. Floating aimlessly in the ocean of floodwater, Waynabozhoo decided that something must be done. He decided to dive down in the water and grab a handful of earth. Waynabozhoo dived down into the depths and was gone for a very long time, returning without the earth. In turn, a number of animals—loon, helldiver, turtle, otter, and mink—all tried and failed. Finally Zhaashkoonh (muskrat) tried. Zhaashkoonh was gone forever, and eventually floated to the surface, dead. Waynabozhoo picked the muskrat out of the water and found a handful of mud in Zhaashkoonh's paw.

Mikinaag (turtle) volunteered to bear the weight of the earth on her back and Waynabozhoo placed the earth there. Waynabozhoo began to sing. The animals danced in a clockwise circular fashion and the winds blew, creating a huge and widening circle. Eventually, they created the huge island on which we live, North America.[104]

Although I have heard this story a number of times, I wasn't able to relate it to resurgence without the help of Edna Manitowabi. In her retelling of it, she asks us to think of ourselves as Zhaashkoonh, the muskrat. This emphasizes the idea that we each have to dive down to the bottom of the vast expanse of water and search for our own handful of earth. Each of us having to struggle and sacrifice to achieve re-creation is not an easy process. We each need to bring that earth to the surface, to our community, with the intent of transformation. Colonization has shattered the fabric of our nation to such an extent that each of us must be Zhaashkoonh; each of us must struggle down through the vast expanse of water to retrieve our handful of dirt.

Once we have brought our paw full of dirt to the surface, it is then our responsibility to also ensure that our action is collectivized. We need to ensure that the other members of the community act on our actions and carry the vision forward. Resurgence cannot occur in isolation. As the animals danced the new world into existence on the turtle's back, the land grew into a large island. It also demonstrates that we need to ask the implicate order for assistance to re-create. If we are doing our work to the best of our abilities, doorways and opportunities will open to us that previously did not exist. After Mikinaag came forward and volunteered to carry the weight of the world on her back, the implicate order acted such that the earth and the Turtle's back grew into the great expanse of North America, because individual and collective responsibilities had been met. In order to dance a new world into existence, we need the support of our communities in a collective action. This story tells us everything we need to know about resurgence. Together, we have all of the pieces. In Nishnaabeg thought, resurgence is dancing on our turtle's back; it is visioning and dancing new realities and worlds into existence.

Resurgence, Wiindigo[105] and Gezhizhwazh

Another series of stories that teaches us about resistance and resurgence are the Wiindigo stories. Wiindigo—a large monster-like creature that is cannibalistic—is one of the characters in Nishnaabeg worldview that embodies imbalance and unhealthy relationships. According to Elder Basil Johnston, Wiindigo craved human flesh, and the more it ate, the more it wanted. Wiindigo had an insatiable hunger for human flesh and was created in times of great hunger, when the temptation to eat human flesh was the greatest. Metaphorically, according to Johnston, Wiindigo stories were designed to prevent cannibalism, but also symbolizes the potentially addictive part of the human condition—when certain desires are indulged, this stimulates more indulgence until all reason and control are lost.[106]

For our ancestors, Wiindigo represented a serious and specific danger in the winter months. More generally, the Wiindigo concept also warns against greed, excesses, and engaging in relationships in which indulgence leads to even more indulgence (various forms of addiction), creating realities based on imbalance. Being greedy and doing greedy things is counter to the promotion of life. Greed creates imbalances as the needs and desires of an individual are put ahead of the well-being of the collective.[107]

In contemporary times, Wiindigo is often used to refer to colonialism and its capitalist manifestations, particularly around natural resources. The state is seen as having an insatiable hunger for natural resources, to the point where it will eventually destroy itself through over-exploitation. This resonates with Indigenous Peoples who read this as cannibalistic. When one harms the earth, one harms oneself because we are part of that whole. Wiindigo is also used to refer to the physiological effects of colonialism on individuals and communities in terms of creating the need for indulgence in order to mask trauma, cope with one's life, or fill a hole created from a past trauma.

I became interested in Wiindigo stories because I thought that since many Nishnaabeg people readily identify Wiindigo with the greed of the colonizer, that resistance to the Wiindigo might reveal something about resistance in terms of colonialism. While there are many stories about Nishnaabeg resistance to the Wiindigo, there is a group of stories that are particularly interesting to me because the hero of these stories is a young woman known as Gezhizhwazh, "to try to cut."[108] Caroline Anderson, from Pimaymootang (Fairford) First Nation in Manitoba, retells this story about Gezhizhwazh:

Mii iwe aaniish aadizookewin weweni ngii-zazcgaajimotaagoomin naanigodiitg. Daabishkoo ingi Wiindigoog mewinzha gaagii-wiindigoowiwaad 'owe. Ogii-amwaawaan wiiji-anishnaabewiwaan ingi Wiindigoog gaa-inind. Mii-, Gajina na ndaa-dibaajimaag?

Ngoji iidog gii-bi-onji-bagamigoziwag ongo wiindigoog. Mii omaa gii-ayaawag. Gii-ayaagaansiinowag iidog aaniish nishtam ishkoniganensan ono gii-ayaagaansiinowag Anishinaabeg. Mii gaa-izhi bagamiguziitaagowaad ini aya'aa wiindigoo'. Bezhig ikwezensan gii-nawapowag. E-bimi-gojigaamoonaawaad ogii-gaagiishkizhwaawaan. Mii Gojizhwaazh ogii-izhinikaanaawaan.

Mii 'awe Gojizhwaazh, mii aazha ozhigewag imaa ini Anishinaabe' odoodisaawaa' ongo Wiindigoog. Mii ezhianoonaawaad mii 'awe Gojizhwaazh. Gegoo odanoonaawaan jinaajibatwaadaminind ji-awi-gagwedwenid. Ah, ikido iinzan mii a'aw Gojizhwaazh, Wiindigoog ongo gaa-odisinekwaa. Ozhiitaag! Giwii-amwagoowag noo'om gaa-dibikag ikido iinzan. Aazha iinzan ezhi-ozhiitaawaad. Gichi-bagwaanegamig iidog ogii-ayaanaawaa.' Iidog ezhi-ozhitoowaad wedi zhoonzhaakowaabaawajigewag. Bibiindigaawaad ini Wiindigoog ji-biindigeyaaboononid. Zhigwa omaa ogii-nepiiminaanaawaan waagaakwadoon ji-onji-niiwana'waawaad.

Mii aazha geget. Mii goda wiin a'a Gojizhwaazh, Gojizhwaazh bi-giiwen. Gegoo miinawaa giga-inaajim odinaawaan iinzan. Mii aazha Gojizhwaazh gii-ishkwaa-dibaajimod o'o. Miisa eni-izhigiiwebatood. Na, mii zhigo gaa-izhi-ozhiitaakanda'waawaad, mii gaa-izhi-maaji-biindigeyaaboonowaad iidog. Apane iidog akawe bakite'aawaad waagaakwadoon ono Wiindigoo.'

Mii 'iwe gaawn aapiji nimaaminonendanzii aaniin gaa-aniinaadizookaagoowaang. Mii dash wiin igo "iwe eko-maamikawiyaan i."[109]

Roger Roulette, an Anishinaabeg language expert from Manitoba, translates the story as follows:

> The story goes ... she [Gezhizhwazh] sacrificed herself to be taken by the *Wiindigoo* because they were going toward where the Ojibwe people were living. And there was a band of them. So she thought, if she sacrificed herself to be taken by the *Wiindigoo*, in that way, she'd have an eye on them, of what they were going to do, what their plans were, even though during the time she was with them, they would cut pieces of her and eat parts of her. But in order to save her own people, the Anishinaabe, she would be taken as lunch. And then she knew their plan. So, when she had the chance to go to the Anishinaabe village, she told them what the *Wiindigoo*'s plans were. She wanted to be the first one to strike, and she also showed the Anishinaabe how to kill the *Wiindigoo*. And she's seen as a hero because she was the main killer of *Wiindigoo*. And that's the story.[110]

The Gezhizhwazh stories provide a theoretical foundation for resistance that places strategy and intelligence at the core of the model. Gezhizhwazh was not physically stronger than the Wiindigo, but she was smarter, more cunning, strategic and committed to achieving her goal, and this was done within the ever-changing conditions of the Nishnaabeg cosmology. Meaning for me at least, that it is not impossible to have plans and strategy in the face of injustice. One still must be open to the emergent properties of the flux of the implicate order, aligned with transmotion, and open in all channels to help from other realms of Creation, but strategy and planning are still present. Something our present-day resistance and resurgence movements often lack.

Gezhizhwazh presents us with a powerful, straightforward resistance force that tell us, when the stakes are high, we need to be strategic, have a plan, think in the long term and be ready to sacrifice individually for the greater collective good. Gezhizhwazh stories teach us that in order to resist, one has to first diagnosis and reveal the problem and then prepare a strategic response.

Nanabush Stories[111]

Nanabush or Nanabozho is a prominent being in the Nishnaabeg worldview—teaching us lessons by never learning and representing the ordinary human struggle to live a good life. S/he is cast as a being that is constantly succumbing to his or her own weaknesses, the consequences of which are demonstrated to the Nishnaabeg through countless stories.[112] Nanabozho is also a powerful teacher, our first teacher, the first researcher, the offspring of powerful spirits, who was raised and influenced by his Nokomis. He has given a vast number of gifts to the Nishnaabeg and done a large amount of balancing.[113] He is often called "the Elder Brother" in English when Nishnaabeg people want to refer to him—demonstrating our kinship with being and also the affection that exists between us.[114] Neal McLeod takes on Vizenor's conceptualization of Nanabush as "trickster," a discussion I have heard orally several times from different academics and Elders. I agree with McLeod's critique of the inaccuracies of the word "trickster" when describing Nanabush:

> The proper term is kistêsinaw, which denotes the notion of the elder brother. This instantly assumes a state of kinship and relationship between humans and the rest of creation. It also moves beyond the intersubjective limitations of human-based discourse which has dominated the West. It moves beyond the conceptual straitjacket that the term "trickster" puts wisahkêcâhk [Nanabush] in: the term suggests that this sacred being is little more than a buffoon.[115]

Basil Johnston describes Nana'b'oozoo as:

> ...the youngest son of Ae-pung-ishimook and Winonah. Nana'b'ozoo is the archuman; he means well, but more often than not, he fails because his appetites get the better of him and overcome his higher nature. When he succeeds it is by chance rather than skill or design; it is akin to a miracle. Nana'b'oozoo represents the ordinary human being in his or her daily struggle to discharge his or her duties toward the manitous neighbors, kin, family and Mother Earth. Like many human beings, Nana'b'oozoo blunders and bumbles along.[116]

My own understanding of this is that Nanabush assumes a role of "buffoon" in some instances in order to be an effective teacher. There are a series of stories of Nanabush bumbling along. But there are also stories where Nanibozho exudes vision, brilliance, strategy and power (the re-creation story, the birth of Nanabozho, Nanabozho steals fire, etc.); or Nanabush behaves as our most loving companion, teacher and mentor; as well, Nanabush helps the Nishnaabeg promote life and more life.

While there is a large, living body of Nanabozho stories in the oral tradition, there is a large body of Nanabozho stories textualized and recorded in both English and Nishnaabemowin. Unfortunately, the cultural context within which these stories were told, and the Nishnaabeg values they were designed to communicate, are often lost in recorded versions. Too often, Nanabozho is cast as an authoritarian character who punishes the Nishnaabeg. Too often, the stories reflect Christian values rather than Nishnaabeg ones. Rather than critique and reveal this by engaging in those texts, I've chosen to engage in a Biskaabiiyang context to retell a traditional Nanabush story, one related to the Sugar Bush that embodies the values of gentleness, re-balancing and love.[117]

Ninaatigoog

In the old days, it was important to take care. It was important to nurture, and to love with all of your heart. Our Elder Brother taught us that one. Oowah. He used to walk all over visiting with us, making sure we had enough food, water, medicine. Making sure our kids weren't sick. Making sure we were all getting along. Visiting. Why did we stop visiting?

One ziigwan, long time ago, this story takes place, long time ago. One ziigwan, that Elder Brother is out visiting, walking all around Nishnaabe Aki, comes to the part in the east where the Michi Saagiig Nishnaabeg live, where that gdigaa bzhiw clan lives, in the south. That part. And he comes to their place in the bush, where those ones live. He comes to visit. Oowah. It's a good thing to visit, to take care. It's a good thing to love. He comes to that place where the gdigaa bzhiwag live and he can't find none of them there. No bzhiwoonsag. No fish smoking. No shkode. No wood piles even. Empty dens. So that Elder Brother, he knows something is wrong, something is not right. It's ziigwan. The gdigaa bzhiwag should be mending nets, setting nets, smoking fish. The ice is off the lake. The winter is in retreat. There should be wood piles, fires, but instead, there is nothing.

So that Elder Brother, he goes walking, looking for those gdigaa bzhiwag. He looks by the river. He looks by the lake. He looks in the bush by the rabbit trails. Nothing. He starts to feel scared. He starts to feel real worried. Something's not right. Gdigaa bzhiwag are missing. Elder Brother's heart starts to rip open a bit. His heart starts to beat too fast.

"Calm down," he tells himself, "breath."

Elder Brother sits down and he thinks. He thinks about how much he loves those gdigaa bzhiwag. How he doesn't see them enough. How maybe if he had just come earlier instead of spending so much time hunting with ma'iingan, that this might not have happened. He feels really, really bad. He feels really, really bad in his heart; and his eyes make tears that run down his face onto the snowy ground. Elder Brother sits with that sadness, and then he makes it into something else.

"GDIGAA BZHIWAG! GDIGAA BZHIWAG!"

No answer.

"GDIGAA BZHIWAG! GDIGAA BZHIWAG!"

Still no answer.

Elder Brother gets up onto his feet now, and he starts to do some thinking, and he starts to do some walking, and he starts to do some more looking. And he looks for a long time. Sometimes in a story like this, he looks and right away he finds what he is looking for, but not this time. This time, Elder Brother looks for a long time. Maybe a few days, maybe more than a few days. Not longer than a week though. Not that long.

Because after a few days he see something funny off in the distance, amongst a stand of ninaatigoog. He sees something and first he thinks he is seeing things from all the looking, but as he get closer, he starts to understand. He sees furry feet and furry legs sticking straight up in the air. He gets closer. He sees furry back lying flat on the snowy ground, in fact snowy ground kinda melty now, but furry back don't care. He gets closer. He sees big cat mouth wide open. Like that big cat at the cat dentist.

But that big cat, she's not at the dentist, she's got that ziiwaagmide dripping right into her mouth. That's right. This story takes place so long ago, that those Ancestors do not have to make ziiwaagmide out of sap. Nope. Them ninaatigoog, they give that syrup right out of there bodies, right over to whoever wants to drink it. And those gdigaa bzhiwag, they want to drink it.

Elder Brother looks around the forest. Every tree's the same. Every tree's got its own gdigaa bzhiw lying on its back, feet in the air, mouth really, really wide open, with that maple syrup dripping right in.

"Bozhoo gdigaa bzhiwag!" yells Elder Brother.

Nobody looks up. Nobody answers.

"Bozhoo gdigaa bzhiwag!" yells Elder Brother.

Again, nobody looks up. Nobody answers.

This is worse than I thought, thinks Elder Brother. And he sings, and dances and stomps and yells and nobody even notices. Everybody's still flat on their backs, with their mouths really, really wide open with that ziiwaagmide dripping right in. Oowah, that ziiwaagmide tastes good. That sweet brown syrup. That's good stuff. Oowah. But enough of that, this here is a big problem and Elder Brother's got to think up a big solution.

And sometimes even Elder Brother's got no ideas. But he knows who does. And he decides to go see Nokomis. That old lady will know what to do. That old lady will know what to do to solve this big problem. Gdigaa bzhiwag are going to get sick. Gdigaa bzhiwag are not eating good food, not taking care of each other. Gdigaa bzhiwag are getting weak just lying on their backs with their furry feet up in the air all day. Gdigaa bzhiwag are getting soft in the mind, not thinking ahead, not looking ahead. Everybody's going to get sick if gdigaa bzhiwag gets sick. Everything's going to go in the wrong way. Elder Brother knows this.

So he walks. He walks and walks and walks and walks. And finally he reaches Nokomis's wigwamin.

"Nokomis," Elder Brother yells, "NOKOMIS."

"Holy Jeez," that old lady says, "Why you yelling like that? Why you yelling like I'm not here?"

"Sorry," says Elder Brother, giving her his semaa. He's not used to things being where they're suppose to be. But this one, she's where she's supposed to be. He feels a bit better, and he sits by her fire in her lodge and he explains his problem.

Nokomis just listens. And then she says, "Nahow. Aambe."

Elder Brother does not quite know what is going on. He was hoping for some medicine. He was hoping for a snack. Nokomis always got good snacks. Maybe a good story. Maybe a sleep on that nice warm sleeping mat. Oowah. That is what he needs. Maybe some soup and that warm blanket wrapped around him. Sit by that fire. Get warm. Feel good. Oowah. But here we go. "Aambe," that old lady says and out the door she goes. Elder Brother's not happy. His mkizinan are wet. His feet are sore. He's been out walking for days. But out the door Nokomis goes, so out the door Elder Brother goes.

Nokomis is an old lady, but she's fast, and she's strong and she's all the way down the path by the time Elder Brother gets out of the wigwamin. "Bekaa," yells Elder Brother, "Wait." He thinks he hears her laughing under her breath and she don't slow down. Elder Brother gotta pick up the pace a bit. His feet hurt. "Bekaa," he yells again. But Nokomis pays no attention. She's all the way down the path and around the corner. Elder Brother's not happy; maybe he starts crying a bit. Maybe he's feeling sorry for himself a bit. All this work. No one paying attention. No one taking care of Elder Brother. But Elder Brother don't got no time for feeling sorry. "Aambe," yells Nokomis, and he keeps walking.

He goes around the corner and Nokomis is standing at the bottom of ninaatig. Elder Brother looks back and realizes he's only fifty metres from her wigwamin. Nokomis is already busy though. She tells him to go to the south side of the tree and to make a notch with the axe. Elder Brother does. She makes a shunt out of cedar, and attaches her akik. They hear the heart beat of the liquid dripping into the bucket. Beat. Beat. Beat. Beat. Beat. Beat. Beat.

Elder Brother feels better. Next Nokomis tells Elder Brother to taste that liquid, and Elder Brother gets excited for that sweet, sweet taste of ziiwaagmide. Maybe he did not get a fire, maybe he did not get any soup and that blanket, but Oowah, he's going to get ziiwaagmide.

Except when he dips his finger into that liquid, it isn't ziiwaagmide.

"GAA GAAWIIN!" yells Elder Brother. He can't take it anymore. "This tastes like nbiish."

Nokomis smiles a tricky smile. "Get a hold of your self," she tells him. "Hang onto your shirt, young one. We're not done yet."

She dips her cup into the akik and tells him to drink the sweet water, and then comes that big important part. That part is so important, that those Nishnaabeg still do it today, even though everything nearly got all ruined. Nokomis tells Elder Brother that the sap, the ziisbaakdwaaboo, is medicine. That it cleans us out, cleans our bodies out for spring.

"It's spring cleaning," she says, laughing under her breath.

"Zhagnash thinks that means wash the curtains. Oowah. Washing your curtains don't clean out nothing. Drink ziisbaakdwaaboo every day of Ziisbaakdoke Giizis. Then you'll be ready."

"Ready for what?" asks Elder Brother.

"Ready for what happens next," says Nokomis.

Then she says, "Back to work," and she gets Elder Brother to tap all the trees in her bush. Then she gets him to collect up all the dead wood and chop it into firewood. Then she gets him to make a big fire. Elder Brother's working so hard, he doesn't have time to feel sorry for himself. And makoog, mikoog, waawaashkeshoog, all those wesiinyag help out. Soon everybody's busy, and that Nokomis is smiling a big smile.

And then she shows them how to concentrate that ziisbaakdwaaboo to save all its good for the niibin, and the dagwagin and next bboon. And they work hard with the fire, and the stones, and finally they get their nsimdana buckets of ziisbaakdwaaboo down to one bucket of ziiwaagmide.

And Elder Brother's happy, because he's ready for a big party and after all that work, he knows Nokomis must have a big party up her old lady sleeve.

But them old lady sleeves are tricky and Nokomis don't say anything about no party. She says, "Nahow Elder Brother. Back to gdigaa bzhiwag."

Elder Brother's party face falls right off. He forgot all about gdigaa bzhiwag. And he don't have any solution to his problem, and they're far away. And he needs a party.

"No party," says Nokomis.

He needs a party.

"NO party," says Nokomis.

He was kind of looking forward to a party.

"Life's a party," say Nokomis. "Party down the trail and go make things right with gdigaa bzhiwag."

Elder Brother knows when he's been beat. So he parties down the trail to go make things right with gdigaa bzhiwag. And he walks and walks and walks and walks and he figures maybe them gdigaa bzhiwag have already got things all worked out. After all, how long could you lie on your back with your feet in the air?"

Long time, if you're gdigaa bzhiwag. Long time.

Elder Brother knows this because by the time he gets back, gdigaa bzhiwag are still lying on their backs, feet in the air, mouths wide open.

"Bozhoo gdigaa bzhiwag!" Elder brother yells.

Nobody pays any attention.

Elder Brother figures he got to get tricky at this point. Otherwise, he's going to have to do a whole bunch more walking and he's never going to get any soup or blanket and his feet are still wet. So he gets tricky. And he needs a bucket to get tricky. And he goes out to ziibi and he fills up that bucket and climbs all the way to the top of ninaatig and he pours that bucket down the tree and he goes back and forth and he does this thirty times. One time for every day in Ziisbaakdoke Giizis.

And maybe that's how this story happens. Maybe. Maybe it was nsimdana akikag and maybe it happens this way.

Maybe Elder Brother was way too tired to lug that heavy bucket up that tall ninaatig. And maybe he was way, way too tired to do that thirty times. And maybe he gotta go pee anyway. And maybe he decide to just whip it out when nobody's looking and do a big long thirty-bucket pee down the top of that tree. And maybe he saved himself thirty trips to the river and thirty trips up the tree, and he was a little closer to that soup and that blanket. Maybe it happened that way.

Whatever way it happened, by the time that *water* got filtered all the way through ninaatig, and by the time Elder Brother did every tree in that sugar bush, the ziiwaagmide dripping into the mouths of gdigaa bzhiwag wasn't ziiwaagmide anymore. It was more like nbiish. It was more like tree pee.

And those gdigaa bzhiwag noticed. And their mouths went shut, and their paws went back onto the ground and they walked over to that

Elder Brother to find out what was going on. And now it was Elder Brother's turn to be Nokomis. He told them he needed a big fire. And they all got busy. He told them he needed a big stack of firewood. And they all got busy. He told them he needed soup and a blanket and a foot rub. And they looked a little suspicious, but they all got busy.

Then Elder Brother told them how much he loved them, and how sad he felt when they forgot about the four sacred foods, and their responsibilities to each other, and to the other clans, and to mino bimaadiziwin. Elder Brother drew them in close by the fire, and he told them how important they were. He told them how Gzhwe Mnidoo had made them the most beautiful, caring creatures that ever walked the earth. He told them he wanted them to walk the earth a long, long time with him. He told them he needed them. He told them his heart knowledge and they felt their hearts getting much, much bigger. They felt filled up.

Gdigaa bzhiwag listened with their whole bodies. Then Elder Brother took them to the south side of the tree, put his tobacco down and he showed them how to tap the trees and collect the sap. He showed them how to cleanse themselves every day of Ziisbaakdoke Giizis. He showed them that once the other animals found out what they were doing, everyone would come and help. He showed them how to boil that sweet water down into sweet ziiwaagmide so they could keep that gift all year long.

Gdigaa bzhiwag accepted that gift from Elder Brother. And every year, no matter how hard it is, they make sure their lips taste the sweetness of ziisbaakdwaaboo, even if it is just once. Even if there isn't enough to make ziiwaagmide. They take their kids. They tell the story of Elder Brother. They listen for the heart beat of their mother as that ziisbaakdwaaboo falls into their pails. They cherish the gift given to their Ancestors so long ago; and in their heart knowledge, hidden away in the most precious parts of their beings, they know that ziiwaagmide wasn't the real gift. They know that the real gift was in the making, and that without love, making just wasn't possible.

The telling and retelling of this story, to me, represents a resurgence narrative. Nanabozho diagnoses the problem, seeks out knowledge from his Nokomis, his Elder, works with all aspects of his being to collectivize the problem and its solution and he builds a clan-based, community-based restoration plan, which results in a local resurgence to realign the people with Creation and mino bimaadiziwin.

What it reveals to me is that destruction (although not genocidal destruction) is part of the cycle of life, and that we as theorists and intellectuals cannot just get stuck in the diagnosis or the revelation of the problem. Nishnaabeg thought propels us to be responsible within our individual selves, to vision and dream our way out of the cognitive box of imperialism.

GLOSSARY OF NISHNAABEMOWIN FOR NINAATIGOOG

aambe — come

akik(ag) — pail(s)

bboon — winter

bekaa — wait

bzhiwoonsag — baby bobcats

dagwagin — autumn

gdigaa bizhiw(ag) — bobcat(s)

ma'iingan — wolf

makoog — bears

mikoog — beavers

mkizinan — moccasins

mino bimaadiziwin — good life

nbiish — water

niibin — summer

ninaatig(oog) — maple tree(s)

Nishnaabeg Aki — Nishnaabe territory

Nokomis — grandmother

nsimdana — thirty

semaa — tobacco

shkode — fire

waawaashkeshoog — deer (plural)

wesiinyag — animals

wigwamin — wigwam

zhaagnash — white person

ziibi — river

ziigwan — early spring

ziiwaagmide — maple syrup

Ziisbaakdoke Giizis — March, Sap Moon

ziisbaakdwaaboo — sap

---

94 Edward Benton-Banai, *The Mishomis Book*, Indian Country Communications, Hayward, WI, 1988, 102.

95 Old-time Nishnaabeg.

96 Edward Benton-Banai, *The Mishomis Book*, Indian Country Communications, Hayward, WI, 1988, 90.

97 Edward Benton-Banai, *The Mishomis Book*, Indian Country Communications, Hayward, WI, 1988, 91.

98 Edward Benton-Banai, *The Mishomis Book*, Indian Country Communications, Hayward, WI, 1988, 94.

99   Shirley Williams, Peterborough, ON, January 24, 2007. Edward Benton-Banai defines *chi-bi-moo-day-win* as migration. Differences in their understandings are likely a result of regional dialects, or the diversity inherent in Nishnaabemowin. Fluent speakers often carry different understandings, teachings, and knowledge of word-origins and this diversity is an important part of the language.

100 According to Shirley Williams, "Dancing on the Turtle's Back" or "Dancing on Our Turtle's Back" would be Niimtoowaad Mshiiken Bakonaang in Manitoulin Island or Niimtoowaad Mikinaag Gijiying Bakonaang in a Mississauga dialect. In John Borrows' comments on an early draft of this book, he used the phrase Mikinaak Agij'ayii Niimi, which Shirley identified as a northwestern dialect. Peterborough, ON, December 7, 2010.

101 Sákéj Youngblood Henderson, *First Nations Jurisprudence and Aboriginal Rights: Defining the Just Society*, Saskatchewan Native Law Centre, Saskatoon, SK, 2006, 123; Treaty Elders of Saskatchewan, 33.

102 Doug Williams learned these teachings as *Kokum Dibajimowanan*, literally "Grandmother Teachings," Peterborough, ON, October 26, 2010. They are often referred to as the "Seven Grandfather Teachings" or the Seven Sacred Gifts; see Edward Benton-Banai, *The Mishomis Book*, Indian Country Communications, Hayward, WI, 1988, 67. Vanessa Watts refers to them as *Anishnaabe Gchi-Twaawendamowinan*, the teachings of the Gifts or Principles of the Seven Grandfathers or the Seven Sacred Gifts in *Towards Anishnaabe Governance and Accountability: Reawakening our Relationships and Sacred Bimaadiziwin*, unpublished thesis, Indigenous Governance Programs, University of Victoria, Victoria, BC, 2004, <web.uvic.ca/igov/research/pdfs/Vanessa%20Watts%20-%20 Thesis.pdf>, accessed September 19, 2010. Vanessa indicated she learned the name of these teachings from Shirley Williams, October 28, 2010. I have also seen them called "Niizhwaaswi Kchitwaa Kinomaadiwinan," <www.anishinaabemdaa.com/grandfathers.htm>, accessed October 26, 2010, and the "Seven Ancestor Teachings" in numerous oral contexts.

103 A number of different versions of this story exists, including "The Great Flood" in Edward Benton-Banai, *The Mishomis Book*, Indian Country Communications, Hayward, WI, 1988, 30–36; Basil Johnston, *Ojibway Heritage: The Ceremonies, Rituals, Songs, Dances, Payers and Legends of the Ojibway*, McClelland and Stewart, Toronto, ON, 1967, 13–16; and Thomas Peacock and Marlene Wisuri, *The Good Path: Ojibwe Learning and Activity Book for Kids*, Afton Historical Society Press, Afton, MN, 16–22. Waynaboozhoo is also known as Nanabozho, Nana'b'oozoo and Nanabush. This is an example of an oral story that is only told in the winter.

104 Edward Benton-Banai, "The Great Flood" in *The Mishomis Book*, Indian Country Communications, Hayward, WI, 1988, 30–36.

105 Some Nishnaabeg are very careful to avoid saying "Wiindigo", while in other regions the name is used in conversation

106 Basil Johnston, *The Anishinaubae Thesaurus*, Michigan State University Press, East Lansing, MI, 2007, 18.

107 Neal McLeod, *Songs to Kill a Wihtikow*, Hagios Press, Regina, SK, 2005, 8–9.

108 Roger Roulette, interviewed by Maureen Matthews, CBC *Ideas Transcript*, "Mother Earth," Toronto, ON, June 5, 2003, 6.

109 Caroline Anderson, CBC *Ideas Transcript*, "Mother Earth," Toronto, ON, June 5, 2003, 6–7.

110 Roger Roulette, CBC *Ideas Transcript*, "Mother Earth," Toronto, ON, June 5, 2003, 7. This is also available online at <qspace.library.queensu.ca/html/1974/157/Mother%20Earth.pdf>, accessed December 17, 2010. However, Caroline Anderson's quotes in Nishnaabemowin were not included in this version.

111 Nanabush stories are only told orally in the winter.

112 Nanabush has the power to transform and appears in many different forms in our stories.

113 Basil Johnston, *The Manitous: The Spiritual World of the Ojibway*, Key Porter Books, Toronto, ON, 1995; Basil Johnston, *The Anishinaubae Thesaurus*, Michigan State University Press, East Lansing, MI, 2007, 17; and Edward Benton-Banai, *The Mishomis Book*, Indian Country Communications, Hayward, WI, 1988.

114 "Elder Brother" is also used to avoid saying "Nanabush" or "Nanibozho" in spring, summer and fall by some Nishnaabeg. Others believe that it is fine to speak Nanabush's name in all seasons, but they still avoid telling the stories in the winter.

115 Neal McLeod, *Cree Narrative Memory: From Treaties to Contemporary Times*, Purich Press, Saskatoon, SK, 2007, 97.

116 Basil Johnston, *Anishinaubae Thesaurus*, Michigan State University Press, East Lansing, MI, 2006, 17.

117 I began telling this version of the story to my children every spring when we went to the sugar bush to help our friends make maple syrup. I originally learned the story from a written source, "How the Indians Got Maple Sugar," Ritzenthaler, Robert E., and Pat Ritzenthaler, *The Woodland Indians of the Western Great Lakes*, Milwaukee Public Museum, Milwaukee, WI, 1983. However, I've always retold it in the context of Michi Saagiig Nishnaabeg cultural values, including benevolence, kindness, compassion, humour and non-punitive restoration. Over the years, I began telling this story in the context of my own clan and as a way of teaching children certain words associated with the Sugar Bush. What is presented here then, is my own re-telling of this story. I have attempted to re-tell it in the context of my clan affiliation, my contemporary life and my interpretation of Nishnaabeg thought. This re-telling bears little resemblance to published versions.

Chapter Five

BUBBLING LIKE A BEATING HEART: A SOCIETY OF PRESENCE

Social mobilization, in its most fundamental form, is at the core of Nishnaabeg governance. In the past, scholars have mistakenly characterized Nishnaabeg governance as less complex and less developed than western forms, primarily because it was localized instead of centralized. By this I mean that governance was localized within an individual's self-determination, the self-determination of families, clans and communities, as well as being localized within a given geographical region. Being enmeshed in the cyclical flux of the earth lodge, Nishnaabeg people traveled throughout their localized territories in a seasonal fashion. In dagwagin,[118] people moved to the shores of certain rivers and lakes to harvest mnomiin[119] by conducting ceremonies, dancing, singing, drumming and picking the rice. After ricing and fall fishing were completed, families moved to hunting or trapping grounds where they would work to cache food and supplies for the coming winter months. In the early parts of spring, families moved to Sugar Bushes to collect the sweet water and make it into maple sugar. Next they moved to spring fishing areas, and finally for niibin,[120] they gathered in larger clan and inter-clan assemblies in their summer areas to berry pick, collect medicinal plants, conduct larger ceremonial gatherings and finally, to engage in inter-clan and inter-regional governance. Our lifeway required cyclical and rhythmical movements. Our governance required annual social and political mobilizations in a way that is unknown to centralized state governing systems, to such a degree that mobilization was normative within our political culture. Our system was built upon mobilization, adaptation and the dynamic nature of a fluctuating environment such that individuals, clans and societies within the nation held certain responsibilities to ensure mobilization could occur.

Dissent was also a normal and a critical part of decision-making processes in all levels of social organization. A plurality of individual truths within a common context provided people with the ability to express themselves and their opinions in a way that simultaneously protected the experience of the individual within the consciousness of the collective. In this way, individual dissent could easily and respectfully be encoded within Indigenous political and intellectual traditions. The oral traditions of Indigenous nations are rich with stories of a single dissenting being, influencing and mobilizing the masses. Recall the Re-creation Stories from the previous chapter. After a great flood, Nanabush and all the animals were stuck on a log in the midst of a vast, never ending body of water. After successive animals tried to dive deep to reach some earth, the inhabitants of the log gave up. That is, until one dissenting individual, Zhaashkoonh, begged to try one more time. She was successful, and thus set off a chain of events that led to the creation of this world and a new Nishnaabeg reality. This story is used to teach our people that hearing and considering the opinions of others, even when they differ from those of the collective, is important because often important interventions come from people close to the spiritual world—women, the elderly and children—coming to us through dreams, visions, and ceremony. These are both people and processes regularly discounted in western society.

I worry that framing contestation or contention along with dissent and mobilization serves to further entrench a polarization between "winner" and "looser," which is not only an artificial imposition on Indigenous theories of mobilization, but in turn it also reinforces the colonial order. Dissent is also problematic in the context of colonialism because it frames Indigenous Peoples as a minority in relation to normative colonial "truth."[121] From an Indigenous perspective, we are not dissenting, mobilizing, resisting or creating controversy to "win" superiority or to dominate settler society. We are advocating and building a resurgence in order to provide the best political and cultural context for the lives of our people to flourish. In fact, if you look closely at our traditions around dispute resolution, restorative justice or even international diplomacy through treaty making, our goals have been consistent throughout history: to restore balance, justice and good health to our lands and our peoples and to have good relations with settler governments and peoples based on respect for our sovereignty, independence and jurisdiction over our territories. This requires a disruption of the capitalist industrial complex and the colonial gender system (and a multitude of other institutions and systems) within settler nations by challenging the very foundation of the nation-state and its relationships to the land and Indigenous nations. However, Indigenous thought tempers a nuanced diplomatic approach to disagreements, built upon a gradual emergence of carefully mediated consensus that considers and addresses difference of opinion from within our communities. This approach in no way dilutes Indigenous aspirations for freedom and self-determination, but has always provided a just process for continued reconciliation of our Constitutional orders with that of Canada's. It is a principled and radically different way of being—one that compels us to act against the forces that attempt to assimilate us into the fabric of Canadian society. It also compels us to regenerate processes within our communities to hear a diversity of perspectives, while also building a united front against colonialism.

Transmotion, Emergence and Mobilization

In Michi Saagiig Nishnaabeg territory we have lost two important relatives during the past century, as a result of the construction of the Trent Severn waterway, a system of locks spanning from Lake Ontario, through the interior of our lands, and eventually into Georgian Bay. Before the waterway was built, colonizing the lifeblood of our system of rivers and lakes, many migratory species of fish traveled in and out of our territory in the spring and fall. Chi'Nbiish (Lake Ontario) had a resident population of salmon closely related to Atlantic salmon that traveled through our territories as far north as Stoney Lake.[122] The salmon were a respected and honoured nation within the culture of the Michi Saagiig Nishnaabeg. There is a convergence between the complex ways Nishnaabeg and salmon organize themselves, govern

themselves and mobilize; and that convergence is based on an inti-
mate and inherent relationship within a localized ecological context.
I have always found it interesting that many nations on the east and
west coast that still have the salmon still have their traditional form
of governance.

Eels represented a similar convergence.[123] Travelling through
Lake Ontario from the Atlantic Ocean, eels again travelled as far north
as Atlantic salmon into Stoney Lake. They were a tremendous source
of protein; and in that sense were the base of the economy and the
base of the nation. Their sheer numbers and ability to travel, adapt
and celebrate the flux of the ecological context, the diversity of life
and power of mass mobilization, impressed and informed Nishnaabeg
thinkers. So much so that when one of our people had a vision for a
mass migration from the Atlantic region to the Great Lakes, it resonated with the people because they had already witnessed their relatives completing a similar journey.

This mobilization is the reason we survived the most dangerous
and oppressive parts of the colonial regime, because it stretched us to a
greater degree to learn how to flourish in a greater diversity of environments. As well, it spread our citizens over a larger land mass. This in
itself afforded us some protection from colonialism because it placed
groups of our people in more protected areas, enabling them to carry
forward the language, culture, intellectual and political traditions to
a greater degree than in the south and eastern doorways of our nation. This was part of the political strategy of our ancestors. The Seven
Fires Prophecy told them of the coming genocide. They knew, they
strategized and they prepared. And we exist as Nishnaabeg and Michi
Saagiig Nishnaabeg today because of that vision, strategy and action.

This is a movement, a mobilization, and a migration towards continuous rebirth. Nishnaabe scholar Gerald Vizenor writes:

> The connotations of transmotion are creation stories, totemic
> visions, reincarnation, and sovenance; transmotion, that sense of
> native motion and an active presence, is *sui generis* sovereignty.
> Native transmotion is survivance, a reciprocal use of nature, not a
> monotheistic, territorial sovereignty. Native stories of survivance are
> the creases of transmotion and sovereignty.[124]

This movement in Nishnaabeg thought is expressed through the structure of the language, which utilizes verbs to a far greater extent than nouns. In the pre-colonial daily life of Nishnaabeg people, movement, change and fluidity were a reality. Family groups and clans travelled cyclically throughout their territories based on the thirteen moons of the year, the seasons and their knowledge of cyclical change in the natural world. At certain times of the year, clans would gather for governance, ceremonies and social activities. Leaders emerged as issues did. Society and clan structure expanded and contracted like a beating heart, or working lungs. Centralized government and political structures are barriers to transmotion; this static state is never experienced in nature. Aligned with the natural word, Nishnaabeg people created political, intellectual, spiritual and social lifeways that enabled them to align themselves individually and collectively with the life forces of their territories.

While Nishnaabeg sovereignty was *sui generis*, it was also territorial. Nishnaabeg people were not wandering around vast expanses of land. While the boundaries around that land were much more fluid than that of modern states, there was a territory that was defined by Nishnaabeg language, philosophy, way of life, and political culture. Nishnaabeg concepts of "nation" and "sovereignty" are much different than modern constructs, but they exist and were expressed.

Roronhiakewen Dan Longboat, a Haudenosaunee scholar, discussed this with me in the context of the Gdoo-Nagaanina, a pre-colonial treaty between our two nations.[125] We talked about how the treaty governed the areas of our two overlapping territories. Dan talked about how pre-colonial treaties facilitated the international Indigenous economy. What I took away from our conversation is that "boundaries," in an Indigenous sense, are about relationships. As someone moves away from the centre of their territory—the place they have the strongest and most familiar bonds and relationships—their knowledge and relationship to the land weakens. This is a boundary, a zone of decreasing Nishnaabeg presence as you move out from the centre of the territory. This is a place where one needs to practice good relations with neighbouring nations. Presence is required to maintain those good relationships. Communication is required to jointly care-take this region, which is much wider than a line.

Nishnaabeg citizenship practices were also aligned with this trans-motion. People wishing to immigrate into our nation were granted full citizenship responsibilities, as long as they were willing to live as Nishnaabeg. While our ways did not require them to give up their identity, the expression of that identity was modulated within the web of mino bimaadiziwin. This is also where our customary adoption practices come from—children were and are readily adopted into our communities and raised as Nishnaabeg citizens when individual fami-lies choosing to extend nurturing relationships to them. They are able to carry this citizenship and the responsibilities embedded within that citizenship through their adult lives if they so chose. This approach is strikingly different from both imposed band membership codes based on arbitrary colonial rules for "status," or blood quantum approaches and self-identification. In a sense, it is based on the self-determina-tion of individual families to decide who their family members are; it is an individual choice in terms of maintaining those responsibilities *and* local community acceptance.[126] Community acceptance was de-pendent then upon the individual's commitment to and expression of the values and philosophies of mino bimaadiziwin. One couldn't just "marry in;" the way you conducted yourself and lived your life would dictate the level of acceptance you gained from the community, as well as the level of responsibilities you were given with regards to citi-zenship. Immigration was a lengthy and emergent process, and the self-determination of our families tells us a lot about how this func-tioned on a larger-scale. Adoption and marriage traditions as processes by which our families brought new members into clans, communities and our nation, were the microcosm for citizenship traditions. Because those caring relationships were so often the responsibility of Aunties, Grandmothers, Sisters, Daughters and Mothers, when we have ques-tions about E-Dbendaagzijig,[127] we should be placing women at the centre of these decisions.

While Nishnaabeg thought embodies transmotion and fluidity, it also has emergence in its foundations. Recall in Chapter Three, my discussion of Biskaabiiyang, and Elder Gdigaa Migizi defining it as a "new emergence." In western science, emergence theory is based on the idea that events are not created on a single structure or rule, but that each component and its surroundings (or relationships) creates a complex chain of processes leading to some order. In Nishnaabeg thought these processes are also mediated through the implicate order or the spirit world, and that "complex" chain of reactions is necessarily non-linear. Nishnaabeg thought comes from the land and therefore, it embodies emergence. Nishnaabeg were adept at viewing and aligning themselves with emergent properties of the natural world—be it mass migration in the animal world, behaviour of schooling fish, herds of buffalo, or the patterns of freezing and melting of bodies of water.

This recognition of the inherent emergence of nature developed thought systems that were process- and context-oriented rather than content-driven. In this way of thinking, *the way* in which something is done becomes very important because it carries with it all of the meaning. The meaning is derived from context, including the depth of relationships with the spiritual world, elders, family, clans, and the natural world.

Sákéj Youngblood Henderson writes about these ideas as aligning oneself with the transformation and flux of the implicate order (creation):

> First Nation jurisprudence is preoccupied with changes. Because of the embodied spirits, life forms are always capable of overcoming all the conditions or determinations of their existence. The spirits are never restricted to any particular embodiment, but generate transformations, the rearrangement of the mystery, the restructuring of the realms of the spirit and embodied spirits. The implicate order informing First Nations jurisprudence is based on inclusion rather than on exclusive divisions or dualities. The aim is to be with the flux, to experience its changing forms, to develop a relationship with the forces, thus creating harmony. In First Nations thought, this flux is often translated as the law of circular inaction and represented through teachings, ceremonies, rituals, prayers, stories, songs, song duels, dances, arts symbols and everyday activities.[128]

The goal of life then becomes the maintenance and promotion of good relations within the emergence or flux of the natural world to maintain and promote balance. Looking into Indigenous communities today, urban or rural, privileged or not, it is evident that colonialism has resulted in a perpetuation of unhealthy relationships and imbalance. Biskaabiiyang is an opportunity to engage in a process that begins to rebalance and establish the conditions for good relationships.

Scott Lyons, a Nishnaabe/Dakota scholar from Minnesota, also writes that movement and migration is a primary cultural value of Nishnaabeg peoples:

> The Ojibwe were a people on the move. The Ojibwe envisioned life as a path and death as a journey; even *Ojibwemowin*, the Ojibwe language is constituted by verbs on the move. What does migration produce? As we can see in the story of the Great Migration, it produces *difference*; new communities, new peoples, new ways of living; new sacred foods, new stories, and new ceremonies. The old never dies; it gets supplemented by the new, and the result is diversity.[129]

That difference was embraced within the web of Nishnaabeg consciousness and used to propel and promote life and rebirth. Diversity afforded us some protection against the forces of colonialism because different pockets of our nation were able to continue aspects of their culture and lifeways that others were not.

Nishnaabeg Society: A Society of Presence

When I think back to the pre-colonial lives of my ancestors, the most striking thing about the way they lived is that they were constantly engaged in the act of creating: making clothes, food, shelter, stories, games, modes of transportation, instruments, songs and dances. They created circumstances to commune with the implicate order, and also created the new generation of Nishnaabeg, based on bringing out their personal gifts and creativity. Creating was the base of our culture. Creating was regenerative and ensured more diversity, more innovation and more life. In essence, Indigenous societies were societies of doing; they were societies of presence. Our processes—be they political, spiritual, education or healing—required a higher degree of presence than modern colonial existence.

In the space of the modern empire, society is a culture of *absence* because consumer culture requires both absence and wanting things in order to perpetuate itself. Without wanting, consumer culture simply cannot exist. In terms of representation, modern society primarily *looks* for meaning (in books, computers, art), whereas Indigenous cultures engage in processes or acts to create meaning. Indigenous cultures understand and generate meaning through engagement, presence and process—storytelling, ceremony, singing, dancing, doing. The re-creation story of dancing on our turtle's back means that creation requires presence, innovation and emergence. It also requires the support of the spiritual world: the process of doing or making is one way that the spiritual world intervenes (through dreams). Making aligns us with our Creation and Re-creation Stories because we begin to act. We use the creative, innovative intelligence imparted to us by Gzhwe Mnidoo to create and voice our truths, to strategize our response, and ultimately to act in creating new and better realities. Creating aligns us with our Ancestors because when we engage in artistic or creative processes, we disconnect ever so slightly from the dominant economic system and connect to a way of being based on doing, rather than blind consumption.

Bubbling Like a Beating Heart

The river that runs through the city I live in is called the Otonabee. The Otonabee runs through Michi Saagiig Nishnaabeg territory from the river we call Zaagaatay Igiwan[130] into Pimaadashkodeyong.[131] In and around Nogojiwanong,[132] the name Otonabee is spoken every day by those of us living in the city—"Best Western Otonabee Inn," "Otonabee Meat Packers," "Otonabee Animal Hospital," and so on. Thousands of times a day, the word "Otonabee" is spoken by people who have no idea what the word means, and who are ignorant of both the history of this Michi Saagiig Nishnaabeg land they live on, as well as our contemporary Michi Saagiig Nishnaabeg presence. This process is repeated all over Canada every day, and represents a kind of disappearance of Indigenous presence.

If you look up the "Otonabee River" in Wikipedia, the site will tell you that the river is called Odoonabii-Ziibi or the Tulibee River.[133] However, there is no reference to where that translation comes from.

I asked my Elder Gdigaa Migizi what the word Otonabee means in Nishnaabemowin. He began by telling me that the first part means "heart," coming from the word *ode*; and the word *odemgat* means boiling water, because when water boils, it looks like the bubbling or beating of a heart. He then explained that Otonabee is an anglicized version of Odenabe—the river that beats like a heart in reference to the bubbling and boiling waters of the rapids along the river.[134]

After I left Gdigaa Migizi's house, I began to think about what the word *ode* means to me as a Michi Saagiig Nishnaabekwe. I thought of how *oodena* means city in our language, and one interpretation of the conceptual meaning of that word is "the place where the hearts gather."[135] I thought about how Odemin Giizis is June, or the moon when the heart berries (strawberries) are ready. I pictured those odeminan, or heart berries, and their runners connecting the plants in a web of inter-relationships, much like cities. I then remembered that, according to Nishnaabeg Elder Basil Johnston, *Odaenauh* refers to nation, which lead me to think of our nation as an interconnected web of hearts.[136] On a deeper philosophical level, that heart knowledge represents our emotional intelligence, an intelligence that traditionally was balanced with physical, intellectual and spiritual intelligence to create a fully embodied way of being in the world. Emotional intelligence or presence on its own, however, is a vital force in Nishnaabeg consciousness. As Nishnaabeg Elder Jim Dumont often explains, our word for truth, (o)debwewin, literally means "the sound of the heart."[137] For Nishnaabeg people then, truth is a personal concept based in love and the raw resonance of emotion. This is just the beginning of the cultural meaning around ode; there are songs, teachings, stories and ceremonial meanings that deepen these basic understandings.

For instance, Nishnaabe Elder Lillian Pitawanakwat from Birch Island (Whitefish River First Nation) tells the story of the origins of heart berries when she explains the e-bngishmog (western direction). She tells of a time when there was a lot of conflict in a community, to the point that one family decided to move deep into the bush to raise their two young boys. The boys grew up play fighting, and after their mother asked them to stop, they secretly continued fighting in the bush. That is, until one day, the younger of the two fell to the ground, banging his head on a rock and dying. The older brother concealed his death and carried the pain of this trauma for many years. Eventually, tiny odeminan began to grow at the grave and the older brother was able to finally let go of his shame, blame, anger and grief over the events that transpired so many years ago.[138] The heart berries serve as a reminder of the importance of working together in a good way, the importance of working through conflict in a manner that doesn't hurt one another, and the importance of letting go. Odeminan remind us of the destructive nature of conflict and of the value of peace. They remind us that the heart is the compass of life and the things that really matter in life are relationships, knowledge and experiences of the heart. So in using oodena as our word for city, the word reminds us of the importance of keeping peace when we gather in large numbers. Our nation is about the promotion of peace.

My point in writing this is that the word "Otonabee" is heard or read differently by Canadians and Nishnaabeg peoples. When I hear or read the word "Otonabee," I think "Odenabe," and I am immediately connected to a physical place within my territory and a space where my culture communicates a multi-layered and nuanced meaning that is largely unseen and unrecognized by non-Indigenous peoples. I am pulled into a Nishnaabeg presence, a decolonized and decolonizing space where my cultural understandings flourish. I am connected to Nishnaabeg philosophy and our vast body of oral storytelling. I am pulled into my Michi Saagiig Nishnaabeg lands, and the beating heart river that runs through it. My consciousness as a Michi Saagiig Nishnaabeg woman, a storyteller and a writer comes from the land because I am the land. Nishnaabemowin seamlessly joins my body to the body of my first mother; it links my beating heart to the beating river that flows through my city. Just as the word *odenabe* pulls me inward, I want my writing and my creative work to do this same thing for others—to pull people into my consciousness as a Michi Saagiig Nishnaabekwe. I want to pull people into a Michi Saagiig Nishnaabeg-constructed world, if even just for a few seconds.

Creating Decolonized Time and Space

Price Chopper is a downtown store that I would bet every Nishnaabeg person in Peterborough and the surrounding reserve communities has been inside to shop for groceries. In 2010, as part of the Ode'min Giizis festival in Peterborough, it became a transformative site.

Nishnaabe curator Wanda Nanibush brought together international Indigenous performance artists and local storytellers as part of an exhibition entitled *Mapping Resistances*. The purpose of the exhibition was to re-map Peterborough from an Indigenous perspective as a way of marking the twentieth anniversary of the "Oka Crisis." *Mapping Resistances* drew attention to how Indigenous Peoples interact with space in cultural and political ways and attempted to address the continual colonial mapping and erasing of Indigenous presence within this space.[139] Wanda writes that performance art, because it is based on process, contradiction, action and connection, is closer to Indigenous ideas of art and resistance. The meaning of both performance art and Indigenous thought is obtained through collective truths that are derived from the experience of individuals, relationships and connections (to the non-human world, the land and each other) through action or "presencing," and through creative process. In line with the Creation Story presented earlier, Wanda writes that this knowledge is created and communicated through the movement of body and sound, testimony and witnessing, remembering, protest and insurrection, by creating a space of storied presencing, alternative imaginings, transformation, reclamation—resurgence.[140]

Rebecca Belmore is a well-known Nishnaabe performance artist who participated in *Mapping Resistances*. Belmore's piece engaged her full body of knowledge as she performed the intervention in a central location in downtown Peterborough.[141] I was an audience member in her performance, which followed my participation in *Mapping Resistances* as an Oral Storyteller.

Belmore's presence was a political, intellectual, spiritual and emotional innovation strategically designed to infuse a colonial space with non-authoritarian power, presence and connection. The entrance to Price Chopper faces a large parking lot, and along the sidewalk is a long, large, brown concrete wall. The audience gathered across the street facing the wall. After a short while, Belmore and two other people—a Nishnaabeg woman and a white man with a trumpet dressed in historic military uniform—drove a black pick-up truck blaring classic rock music up onto the side walk. Belmore got out of the truck and methodically placed four purple pillows on the sidewalk with four rocks on each pillow. She then proceeded to unload dozens of single litre plastic bags of milk and lined them between the pillows. When the milk was lined up, she aggressively and violently ripped open each bag with her teeth, and filled up a large bucket. When all the bags were open, she took a long paint roller and began to paint three large Xs on the brown concrete wall. The other Nishnaabeg woman methodically washed each X off with a garden hose, while the military man played sad music on his trumpet. This went on for several minutes. Presencing and erasing. Eventually, the three packed up their belongings, hosed off the sidewalk and left in the black truck.

The performance itself was dense, with references to other work (including the other festival performances) and Nishnaabeg metaphor: colonizers have taken our land and our sustenance, and through the processes of capitalism, industry and manufacturing, they have used our own sustenance, represented as milk, to erase. However, my focus here is the transformative nature of the performance in terms of space. Witnessing Belmore's performance was an extraordinarily meaningful experience in my life, one that I have thought of almost everyday since it happened. During the performance I felt powerful, free, and inspired. I felt proud of who I am. Belmore drew me into a decolonizing space where my presence and attention became completely focused in a similar fashion to what happens during natural childbirth, or ceremony. I lost sense of time and space. I was transported into a world that Belmore as the artist/storyteller had envisioned—a world where Nishnaabeg flourished and where justice prevailed, a world where my voice and my meanings mattered. Downtown Peterborough, like any other occupied space in the Americas, is a bastion of colonialism as experienced by Nishnaabeg people. But for twenty minutes in June, that bastion was transformed into an alternative space that provided a fertile bubble for envisioning and realizing Nishnaabeg visions of justice, voice, presence and resurgence.

It reminded us that we as Nishnaabeg people are living in political and cultural exile. Yet, it disrupted the narrative of normalized dispossession and intervened as Nishnaabeg presence—not as a victim, put as a strong non-authoritarian Nishnaabekwe power. Belmore's performance was liberation from within; and I am reminded of her/my presence, her/my power because she has altered the landscape in my memory and in the memory of everyone who witnessed her performance. Nishnaabeg and Indigenous artists like Belmore interrogate the space of empire, envisioning and performing ways out of it. Even if the performance only lasts twenty minutes, it is one more stone thrown in the water. It is a glimpse of a decolonized contemporary reality; it is a mirroring of what we can become. That day, Rebecca Belmore was my modern day Gezhizhwazh.

---

118 Autumn.

119 Wild rice.

120 Summer.

121 Thanks to Christine Sy for pointing this out to me in a previous draft.

122 Doug Williams, guest lecture, INDG 3630, Trent University, Peterborough, ON, November 9, 2009.

123 I first asked Doug Williams if he knew the word for Eel. He couldn't remember, so he called his Auntie and Uncle at Curve Lake, October 26, 2010. They remembered the word as *mgizi*—very close in pronunciation to *migizi*, the word for eagle. Shirley Williams, after consultation with other fluent speakers, came up with *naag-bwe* for lamprey eels, November 25, 2010.

124 According to Gerald Vizenor, "[n]ative *sovenance* is that sense of presence in remembrance, that trace of creation and natural reason in native stories; once an obscure noun, the connotation of sovenance is a native presence in these essays, not the romance of an aesthetic absence or victimry." Gerald Vizenor, *Fugitive Poses: Native American Indian Scenes of Absence and Presence*, University of Nebraska Press, Lincoln, NB, 1998, 15.

125 Roronhiakewen Dan Longboat, Peterborough, ON, March 8, 2010.

126 For a discussion of how individual families exercised this in the context of adoption and family law by extending relationships of caring to outsiders, see Donald Auger, *The Northern Ojibwe and Their Family Law*, unpublished dissertation, Osgoode Hall Law School, York University, Toronto, ON, 2001, 179. Anishnaabek scholar Darlene Johnson also notes that this process adapted to colonial disruptions in the territoriality of our clan system by requiring those marrying and moving to live in another clan's region to ask permission before moving. Oral presentation, Inclusion and Representation in Anishinabek Self-Government Conference, Nipissing First Nation, January 21–22, 2011.

127 *E-Dbendaagzijig*, "those who belong," a term used by the Anishinabek nation as a citizenship code.

128 Sákéj Youngblood Henderson, *First Nations Jurisprudence and Aboriginal Rights: Defining the Just Society*, Native Law Centre, University of Saskatchewan, Saskatoon, SK, 2006, 153.

129 Scott Lyons, X *Marks: Native Signatures of Assent*, University of Minnesota Press, Minneapolis, MN, 2010, 4.

130 This is now known as the Trent River. The traditional name means that the river is shallow. Doug Williams, Waawshkigaamagki (Curve Lake First Nation), July 15, 2010.

131 This is now commonly known as Rice Lake. *Pimaadashkodeyong* means the lake beside the burning plains or prairie. Doug Williams, Waawshkigaamagki (Curve Lake First Nation), July 15, 2010; Rick Beaver, Alderville First Nation, October 14, 2008; and Ruth Clarke, *To Know This Place: The Black Oak Savana/ Tallgrass Prairie of Alderville First Nation*, Sweet Grass Studios, Alderville First Nation, ON, 2005.

132 Peterborough, the place at the foot of the rapids.

133 Accessed September 11, 2010, <en.wikipedia.org/wiki/Otonabee_River>.

134 Doug Williams, Waawshkigaamagki (Curve Lake First Nation), July 15, 2010.

135 Language expert Anton Treuer writes, "The word *doodem* comes from the morpheme *de*, meaning 'heart or center.' The relationship between the words *ode'* (his heart), *oodena* (village), *doodem* (clan), and *dewe'igan* (drum) has caused considerable confusion among some scholars, who have occasionally claimed that one of these words was derived from another when in fact they simply share the same root morpheme *de*. *Ode'* (the heart) is the centre of the body, *Oodena* (the village) is the center of the community, and *doodem* (the clan) is the center of spiritual identity. *Dewe'igan* (the drum) is the centre of the nation, or its heartbeat," *The Assassination of Hole in the Day*, Borealis Books, St. Paul MN, 2011, 15. Doug Williams understands *oodena* as being derived from the verb *daawe*—to buy or sell. Peterborough, ON, November 30, 2010. Norbert Hardisty (Hollow Water First Nation), however, remembers an Elder from Minnesota (Porky White, Leech Lake) explaining to him "oodena as being derived from the verb to buy and sell or commerce," but he also remembers his Grandmother, a fluent speaker and Elder from Hollow Water First Nation in Manitoba, explaining to him that *oodena* was derived from g'debwe. She understood *oodena* to mean "the place where the hearts gather." Hardisty knew and felt comfortable with both interpretations of the origin and meaning of the word. Hollow Water First Nation, Manitoba, December 6, 2010. Edna Manitowabi also shared this understanding and origin of the word *oodena*, January 20, 2011, North Bay, ON. Basil Johnston also groups the words *Odae-meen* (strawberry), *n'd'odaem* (my family—the heart of my being, or where my heart belongs my clan; my clan symbol), *ningo-d'odaewiziwin* (a single family; the distended family), *odaenuh* (a town) and *odaenauh* (a nation) under *Odae* (heart), indicating the words are related. Basil H. Johnston, *Anishinaubae Thesaurus*, Michigan State University Press, East Lansing, MI, 2007, viii-ix , 178.

136 Basil H. Johnston, *Anishinaubae Thesaurus*, Michigan State University Press, East Lansing, MI, 2007, 178.

137 Jim Dumont, Elders' Conference, Trent University, Peterborough, ON, February 20, 2010.

138 To hear Lillian Pitawanakwat tell this story, click on "Ojibwe" and then "west" at <www.fourdirectionsteachings.com>, accessed September 12, 2010.

139 Wanda Nanibush, *Mapping Resistances*, curatorial essay, Peterborough, ON, 2010, 2.

140 Wanda Nanibush, *Mapping Resistances*, curatorial essay, Peterborough, ON, 2010, 2.

141 Belmore's performance took place on June 19, 2010, in Peterborough, ON.

Chapter Six

RESURGENCE IN OUR POLITICAL RELATIONSHIPS

Echoes from the Past

Within the Dibaajimowinan of individuals and families, there is a wealth of oral stories and memories where all kinds of acts of hidden and not-so-hidden resistance have occurred throughout time. These acts or stories involve parents teaching their kids the language or a song, Mothers and Aunties working so hard to keep their children fed and cared for in the face of poverty, oppression and often violence, as well as individuals standing up for themselves or their loved ones in stores, government agencies, schools, hospitals, nursing homes, jails, courts, banks and doctors' offices. Although these acts may not have catalyzed large-scale mobilizations, or perhaps even brought about discernable immediate change, nevertheless they have influenced Indigenous presence enough that the stories were passed along. These are acts of individuals throwing their stone in the water and they exist in every family. They are often humorous and always engaging. They are stories of *survivance*, as Vizenor would say.

Writing broadly about Indigenous resistance in Canada, Kiera Ladner and myself wrote the following in an attempt to broaden conceptualizations of resistance to include all the mechanisms, processes and actions that prevent Zhaaganashiiyaadizi and to emphasize that as long as their has been colonialism on our lands, there has been resistance.

> The Ancestors not only fought, blockaded, protested and mobilized against these forces on every Indigenous territory in Turtle Island, they also engaged in countless acts of hidden resistance and kitchen

table resistance aimed at ensuring their children and grandchildren could live as *Indigenous* Peoples. The Grandmothers, Mothers and Aunties were particularly adept at keeping us alive, and passing down whatever traditions they could so we would have warmth in our hearts and warmth in our bellies. We believe it is important to reveal the legacy of resistance in order to not only shatter mainstream Canada's image of Indigenous Peoples as "passive victims" of colonization, but also to demonstrate to future generations that they exist because of the responsibility, sacrifice, courage and commitment of their Ancestors.[142]

From my perspective as a Nishnaabekwe, whenever one throws a stone into the lake with intent, commitment and vision, the implicate order or spiritual world mobilizes to provide support and open doors. The emergent nature of Nishnaabeg mobilization, resistance and resurgence means that it is impossible to predict which stones will cascade through time and space, producing impacts, shifts, and transformations. Kiera Ladner, writing about the profound impact of the "Oka Crisis" on her generation emphasizes that Indigenous mobilizations throughout history start with little things:

> There have been and will continue to be countless seemingly "little things from which big things grow" on Turtle Island. Little things like the message of peace, power and righteousness that Hiawatha and the Peacemaker promoted among the Onkwehonwe and which became the foundation of the Great Law of Peace and the creation of a confederacy of nations founded on this message (the Haudenosaunee). Little things like Mistahimaskwa refusing treaty, citing the need for meaningful and trustworthy consultation and negotiation and reminding the representatives of the Crown that the Nehiyaw are a sovereign people, who will not (and have not) ceded their right to self-determination nor their territories, which they agreed to share with the newcomers. Little things like the women (including Sandra Lovelace, Jeannette Corbière Lavell and Irene Bédard) who refused to leave and/or returned to their reserves after they had married non-status men, gotten divorced or been widowed and who brought this gendered inequality to the streets, the Canadian Courts, the constitutional talks, the United Nations and the International Court of Justice. Little things like all of those

parents and grandparents who refused to allow the state/church to take their kids to residential school and fought tirelessly for day schools, access to high school, integration and band-controlled education. Little things like Frank Calder and the Nisga'a Nation taking the Canadian Government to court in the 1970s in defense of their land rights and Aboriginal Title. Little things like all those fishermen (and women) like Dorthy Van der Peet and Donald Marshall Jr. who struggled for years on their rivers, their lakes and their oceans to maintain their fisheries despite being told that they were "fishing illegally" and knowing that they would end up in Canadian jails and courts. Little things like the Dene Declaration of 1975 and the corresponding mobilization of the nation in defense of their homelands. Little things like:

The echoes of these past resistances continue to be heard. I am sure that the echoes of past were heard that March at Kanehsatà:ke when a group of people decided to quietly block a dirt road in their community to raise awareness of the local golf course's intention of developing their community commons (a piece of land that had been claimed as part the Kanien'kehaka community from the outset when the Kanien'kehaka established that community and started to bury their people in those now iconic pines on the commons). Given that this was not the first attempt to have settler governments deal with the very same land issue that defined the 1990 resistance and given that this was not the first flashpoint or episode of mobilization in Kanehsatà:ke, I am quite certain echoes of the past were heard that summer as the Ancestors stood shoulder to shoulder with the generations of today.[143]

Echoes of past resistance come to the present through dreams, visions and Dibaajimowinan. Storytelling is one mechanism through which Biskaabiiyang operates. Cree scholar, poet and visual artist Neal McLeod explains, "The 'echo' metaphor has often been used by Cree storytellers as a way of describing the past coming up to the present through stories."[144] I often think of Dibaajimowinan as the stones our Ancestors cast in the lake, echoing or reverberating out through time and space into the present. Things my great-great-great-Grandmother did and choices she made contribute to who I am and how I live in the world today. The stories I have of her influence my life. The *telling* of these stories in Nishnaabeg contexts — meaning oral contexts where contemporary Nishnaabeg cultural practices are the norm—is an act of Nishnaabeg presence and as Vizenor would say, transmotion.

Storytellers skilled in specific Indigenous cultural traditions weave narratives together in a particular way based on the audience themselves and their response to her or his presence. Neal McLeod writes that there is also a critical reflection or examination that is woven into the experience for both the storyteller and the audience.[145]

Meaning is derived from the presence of both the storyteller and the listeners. Storytelling is an emergent practice, and meaning for each individual listener will necessarily be different. The relationships between the storyteller and the listeners become the nest that cradles the meaning. The storyteller creates both the context and the content and collectively a plurality of meanings are generated through the experiences of the audience. The "analysis" and the "critical examination" are done with the utmost care and respect. Nishnaabeg storytellers, when telling in English, will use phrases such as "maybe it happened this way," "some people say that's what happened, I don't know, I wasn't there" or "I heard it happened that way, but I don't know." Revealing that one can only speak about what they know to be true from direct experience. The "critical examination" follows the protocols of Aanjigone with phrases such as "this is when my big mistake happened" or "this time in my life I was flying in circles."

The process for integration into the experience of the storyteller and the audience is one that is slow in comparison to western standards. It can take many years after hearing a story to know the meaning of that story in one's heart—for it to become a truth—yet the process of it becoming heart-knowledge or Debwewin is the process of integrating that echo into one's experience. This is critical in a Biskaabiiyang context because our Elders are constantly telling us (particularly writers and academics) that one has to live the knowledge in order to know it. McLeod recalls a story that reminded me of this:

> The late Jim Ka-Nipitehtew, an elder from Onion Lake, said that what he knew was like an "echo of older voices from a long time ago." Once, when Edwin Tootoosis was visiting my father, he told me "moy e-kistawet" ("it does not echo"). He was referring to the land, and the fact that the land no longer had sound in the same way it had before.[146]

If we do not live our stories and our teachings, the echoes become fainter and will eventually disappear. When the land is not being used in a respectful and honourable away, the power of her teachings are lost. Healers know that plants will disappear if one takes too much, and also if one does not use them at all. The more we tell stories, the more stories there are to tell, the more echoes that come up to the present. In the old days, stories connected our families to one another; they stitched together our collective consciousness; they stitched together our nation.

I have been telling stories informally within my family and my community since my children were born. I began telling stories to them as a way of telling them about myself, our family, our community and our culture. Storytelling then grew for me, and I began using it as a way of teaching in the university classroom, and at local cultural events. What follows is one of my Dibaajimowinan related to the birth of my two children, Nishna and Minowewebeneshiinh. Both my children were born at home under the care of midwives so that I could participate fully in the ceremony of giving birth and ensure that entrance into this world was as gentle, loving and following Nishnaabeg traditions of birth as much as possible. I have breastfed children continuously for the past eight years. These three experiences (the two births and the breastfeeding) have had a profound impact on my being, as has mothering. As an intellectual, I've wanted to write about these experiences because I have learned a great deal through these engagements, but it has been difficult. I have been asked to remove sections talking about breastfeeding because they are irrelevant to the academic work I was discussing. I have also been asked by Native women academics to remove the academic components of papers discussing birth and breastfeeding because only the actual birth narratives were relevant. This leaves me to believe that there it is still pressure to separate theory and academics from Dibaajimowinan and the personal, despite the fact that Dibaajimowinan are recognized as a valued and important source of knowledge within Anishinaabe-gikendaasowin.[147]

Biskaabiiyang means that new stories often come from old stories. Breastfeeding as an act of nourishing is a prominent part of our Creation Story. There are some very old stories about how Michi

Saagiig Nishnaabeg people relate to our land and our neighboring nations, ones that I would like to share because I believe that those old stories hold the beginnings to the new stories we are about to create. Thinking about those old stories, dreaming and visioning a different future, those are the seeds that we will use to plant our new garden. As it is so often in my culture, the old story this time begins with the women.

Breastfeeding and Treaties

About seven years ago, I offered Edna Manitowabi some tobacco and asked her to guide me through my first pregnancy and birth. Edna is an Elder and a Grandmother and one of the Spiritual leaders of our nation. She taught me a lot of things; and her teachings got my two children safely through the doorway and into this world. But it was her teachings about nursing and breastfeeding that got me thinking about treaties in a much different way than I had before.

Canadians are taught that treaties are legal agreements through which Indians ceded our lands for cash. The Canadian characterization of treaties is almost like a receipt for a business transaction. From the perspective of the Canadian state, treaties are about obtaining title to our lands "legally," or at least "legally" according to the traditions of the British legal system. Indigenous Peoples, however, have a different perspective on the meaning of those treaties and we have a different history in treaty making. At the time of contact we had been making treaties with animal nations and with other Indigenous nations for generations. Like our other political traditions, the family was the teaching ground for these understandings, with women carrying the responsibility for first sharing these teachings with our youngest citizens.

Breastfeeding is the very first treaty. Edna explained to me that breastfeeding is where our children learn about treaties, the relationships they encode and how to maintain good treaty relationships. Of course as someone who didn't have children at the time and who had never nursed, I had absolutely no idea what she was talking about.

When my first child Nishna came along, I started to understand. Nursing is ultimately about a relationship. Treaties are ultimately about a relationship. One is a relationship based on sharing between a mother and a child and the other based on sharing between two sovereign nations. Breastfeeding benefits both the mother and the child in terms of health and in terms of their relationship to each other. And treaties must benefit both sovereign independent nations to be successful.

When my second child Minowewebeneshiinh came into our lives, she brought with her a deeper understanding of these teachings. She taught me about balance—that if relationships get out of balance, then that imbalance can effect the health and wellness of the mama and the baby. She taught me that those early years set the tone for the entire relationship. That's why that time is so important and we have to be so careful and so gentle with our children. Minowewe taught me that both the mother and the child have to be taken care of, in order for the relationship to work. So in treaties, the relationship must be one of balance. One nation cannot be dominant over the other. One nation cannot control all of the land and all of the resources. Those early days were important, when our peoples were first meeting, because they set the tone for the relationship between the Nishnaabeg nation and the Canadian state—a relationship that hasn't changed very much at all in contemporary times.

Three years ago, I became an Auntie for the first time. And little Aanjinokomi once again deepened my understanding of our first treaty. I had been nursing at this point for nearly seven years, so I thought that I was some sort of an expert, but Aanjinokomi brought me some humility. For me, the beginning of the nursing relationship had come easily; but not for my sister. She was in lots of pain and feeling very overwhelmed. The latch wasn't quite right, and it was partly my responsibility to help the two of them negotiate their new relationship. My family had been back and forth and back and forth from Toronto so that I could sit with her, help her get positioned properly, help her get his mouth opened wide enough. And so the teachings were deepened. Aanji taught me that negotiating treaty is about patience and persistence. It is about ensuring the relationship for the long term. The relationship comes first above all else, above the pain. It is about commitment and compassion. It is about a love of the land

and a love for the people. And it requires the support of your family and your community. Treaties cannot be maintained without the support of your family, your community and ultimately, the nation.

Before there were humans on earth, a female spirit being came to the earth. Her name was Wenonah, which means the first breast feeder—*nonah* is to breastfeed; *we* is "the one who."[148] Wenonah took the responsibility of creating humans on earth. She came to earth, and with struggle, eventually created humans. Nishnaabeg people are her descendants. We exist today because she united with w-bng-ishmog (the west wind) and created the first humans. She created and then nourished us by nursing us.[149] When women breastfeed they are aligning themselves with this sacred story, engaging in the act of creating a new life. Breastfeeding was so important in this Creation Story that Wenonah carries it as her name. To me, this means that as a people, Nishnaabeg have a great deal to learn by being breast-fed, by breastfeeding, and by supporting and honouring breastfeeding women.

This has even greater resonance because for Nishnaabeg people, our political culture begins at home. It begins with nursing and how we parent our kids. In the past, our people practiced a form of governance that was at its core non-hierarchical and non-authoritarian. Our leaders guided our nations not by force or authority, but by following the will of the people. Our leaders were responsible for building consensus amongst the people and they were responsible for the sustainability of the nation.

So these values were reflected in our parenting and in our families. In order to reproduce those qualities prized in a traditional leader, carried in Kokum Dibaajimowinan, our ancestors practiced relationships with children that embodied kindness, gentleness, patience and love. Children were respected as people, they were encouraged to follow their visions and to realize their full potential while living up to the responsibilities of their families, communities and nations. This was the key to creating leaders with integrity, creating good governance, and teaching future leaders how to interact in a respectful manner with other human and non-human nations. My ancestors knew that maintaining good relationships as individuals, in families, in our nation and internationally was the basis for lasting peace. This was the foundation of mino bimaadiziwin or "living the good life."

Our relationships extend out from the mother and child, through our families, our clans, and our community. They also extend to the land and how we interact with the natural world. Breastfeeding my two children deepened my understanding of Nishnaabeg treaty relationships. The *telling* of this experience then led me to other stories about Nishnaabeg political relationships; and so I want to share with you another old story from this territory about how we relate with the land. A long time ago our clan leaders negotiated particular agreements with animal nations or clans to promote mino bimaadiziwin and balance with the region.

Gchi-dbaakgonigewin[150]

The 1850 Robinson Huron Treaty, covering a region on the north shore of Lake Huron, is referred to in the Nishnaabeg oral tradition as Gchi-dbaakgonigewin — a big law or law-making agreement, but an agreement that is open, with matters to be added.[151] From the perspective of Indigenous Peoples, treaties were viewed as sacred relationships between independent and sovereign nations, including agreements between humans and non-humans.[152] The land specifically reminds me of these relationships. For example, in Michi Saagiig Nishnaabeg territory, the people of the fish clans, who are the intellectuals of the nation, met with the fish nations[153] twice a year for thousands of years at Mnjikanming,[154] the small narrows between Lake Simcoe and Lake Couchiching. The fish clans and the fish nations gathered to talk, to tend to their treaty relationships, to renew life just as the Gzhwe Mnidoo had instructed them. These were important gatherings because the fish nations sustained the Nishnaabeg nation during times when other sources of food were scarce. Fish were a staple in our traditional foodway. Our relationship with the fish nations meant that we had to be accountable for how we used this "resource." Nishnaabeg people only fished at particular times of the year in certain locations. They only took as much as they needed and never wasted. They shared with other members of their families and communities, and they performed the appropriate ceremonies and rituals before beginning. To do otherwise would be to ignore their responsibilities to the fish nations, jeopardizing the health and wellness of the people. In contemporary times, Mnjikanming remains an important place in our territory because it is the place people of the fish clans came and continue to come to renew their relationship with the fish nations. Similarly, Nishnaabeg scholar John Borrows retells one of our sacred stories in *Recovering Canada: The Resurgence of Indigenous Law* and further illustrates the importance of these diplomatic agreements between human and animal nations.[155] A time long ago, all of the deer, moose and caribou suddenly disappeared from the Nishnaabeg territory. When the people went looking for them, they discovered the animals had been captured by the crows. After some negotiation, the people learned that the crows were not holding the moose, deer and caribou against their will. The animals had willingly left the territory because the Nishnaabeg were no longer respecting them. The Nishnaabeg had been wasting animal meat and not treating animal bodies with the proper reverence. The animals knew that the people could not live without them. When the animal nations met in council, the chief deer outlined how the Nishnaabeg nation could make amends, telling the Nishnaabeg that they must honour the waawaashkeshigook in both life and death: by not wasting their flesh; by preserving their habitats; by leaving tobacco to acknowledge the anguish humans have brought upon the waawaashkeshigook in order to feed themselves; and to engage in ceremony to nurture this relationship.[156] The Nishnaabeg agreed and the animals returned to their territory. Contemporary Nishnaabeg hunters, when they kill a deer or moose, still go through the many rituals outlined that day. Judy DaSilva, Nishnaabekwe from Asubpeechoseewagong Netum Anishnaabek (Grassy Narrows) in northwest Ontario, explains how these teachings are still relevant in her community today:

> When a hunter kills a moose, there is a certain part of the moose that the hunter takes off, and leaves in the forest, and with that the hunter will say a few words to thank the moose for providing food for his family. ...My brother said our grandmother told him that you do not get an animal because you are a good hunter, but because the

animal feels sorry for you and gives himself to you to feed your family. This is why when our people hunt, these thoughts are ingrained
in their minds and their hearts and they have great respect for the
animals they get.[57]

According to Nishnaabeg traditions, our relationship with the moose
nation, the deer nation and the caribou nation is a treaty relationship
like any other, and all the parties involved have both rights and responsibilities in terms of maintaining the agreement. The treaty outlines a
relationship that, when practiced continually and in perpetuity, maintains peaceful coexistence, respect and mutual benefit. These are but
two examples of treaties between the Nishnaabeg nation and the nonhuman world, but it serves to illustrate several important Nishnaabeg
values regarding this process. First and foremost, treaties are about
maintaining peace through healthy relationships. They require commitment and work, but when done correctly can bring about a lasting
peace for all involved.

Dewe'igan,[58] the Heartbeat of the Nation

Two years after my son Nishna was born, my sister took me to a drummaking workshop at First Nations House at the University of Toronto.
Steve Teekens taught the group the appropriate teachings for hand
drums, and also told us his version of the following story while we
made our drums.[59]

The Nishnaabeg nation, in addition to living up to their treaty
relationships with the non-human world, also made political agreements with their neighbouring nations. I am reminded of this every
time the ancient teaching of how the drum came to the Nishnaabeg
is retold. In one particular version, the Nishnaabeg nation was in
conflict with the Dakota nation. After several years of strife, a young
woman dreamed or visioned the drum. She was taught several songs
to share with the people. Following her vision, she constructed a
drum, and taught both the Dakota and the Nishnaabeg peoples the
songs. The drum became more than a symbol of peace between the
two nations. By carrying out the ceremonies given to her, and by
sharing them with the people, peace between the two nations has

been maintained ever since.[160] All of these values and processes are reflected in the Nishnaabeg nation's pre-colonial treaty-making practices, and these practices provide us with important insights into the kind of relationship our Ancestors intended to have, and intended us to have with settler governments.

Gdoo-naaganinaa, Our Dish[161]

Gdoo-naaganinaa, meaning "Our Dish,"[162] is another such relationship Nishnaabeg people in the southeastern portion of the territory had with the Haudenosaunee Confederacy.[163] Our Ancestors intended for this relationship to continue perpetually, and it is relevant today because it provides us with a model for building solidarity with our Haudenosaunee neighbours and renewing our ancient and historic friendship. It is also highly relevant in contemporary times because it sets forth the terms for taking care of a shared territory while maintaining separate, independent sovereign nations. Gdoo-naaganinaa acknowledged that both the Nishnaabeg and the Haudenosaunee were eating out of the same dish through shared hunting territory and the ecological connections between their territories.[164] The dish represented the shared territory; although it is important to remember that sharing territory for hunting did not involve interfering with one another's sovereignty as nations. It represented harmony and interconnection, as both parties were to be responsible for taking care of the Dish. Neither party could abuse the resource. It was designed to promote peaceful coexistence and it required regular renewal of the relationship through meeting, ritual and ceremony. The Nishnaabeg nation and the Confederacy related to each other through the practice of Gdoo-naaganinaa. It was not just simply agreed upon, but practiced as part of the diplomatic relations between the Nishnaabeg nation and the Confederacy. All of the nations involved had particular responsibilities to live up to in order to enjoy the rights of the agreement. Part of those responsibilities was taking care of the Dish. Nishnaabeg environmental ethics dictated that individuals could only take as much as they needed, that they must share everything following Nishnaabeg redistribution of wealth customs and no part of the

animal could be wasted.[165] These ethics, combined with their exten-
sive knowledge of the natural environment—including its physical
features, animal behaviour, animal populations, weather and ecological interactions—ensured that there would be plenty of food to sustain
both parties in the future. Decisions about the use of resources were
made for the long term. Nishnaabeg custom required decision mak-
ers to consider the impact of their decisions on all the plant and animal nations, in addition to the next seven generations of Nishnaabeg.
The Haudenosaunee refer to the treaty as the "Dish with One Spoon"
treaty and there is an associated Wampum Belt.[166] The concept behind
the Dish with One Spoon Wampum reflects the principles that were
given to the Haudenosaunee by the Peacemaker in the Kaienerekowa
(Great Law of Peace).[167] Again the Dish represents shared hunting
grounds, but in the Haudenosaunee version there is One Spoon, not
only to reinforce the idea of sharing and responsibility, but also to promote peace. There are no knives allowed around the Dish so that no
one gets hurt.[168] Again, Haudenosaunee people understood the treaty
as a relationship with both rights and responsibilities. Haudenosaunee
land ethics also ensured the health of the shared territory for generations to come.[169]

Gdoo-naaganinaa in Contemporary Times

At no time did the Haudenosaunee assume that their participation
in the Dish with One Spoon treaty meant that they could fully col-
onize Nishnaabeg territory or assimilate Nishnaabeg people into
Haudenosaunee culture. At no time did the Haudenosaunee assume
that the Nishnaabeg intended to give up their sovereignty, independence or nationhood. Both political entities assumed that they would
share the territory, that they would both take care of their shared hunting grounds and that they would remain separate, sovereign, self-de-
termining and independent nations. Similarly, the Nishnaabeg did
not feel the need to "ask" or "negotiate" with the Haudenosaunee
Confederacy for the "right" to "self-government." They knew that
Gdoo-naaganinaa did not threaten their nationhood; Our Dish
was meant to preserve their nationhood, protect their territory and

maintain their sovereignty. At the same time, both parties knew they had a shared responsibility to take care of the territory, following their own culturally based environmental ethics to ensure that the plant and animal nations they were so dependent upon carried on in a healthy state in perpetuity. Both parties knew that they had to follow their own cultural protocols for renewing the relationship on a regular basis to promote peace, goodwill and friendship amongst the Nishnaabeg and the Haudenosaunee. Both parties knew that, if peace were to be maintained, they had to follow the original instructions passed down to them from their Ancestors. Although Gdoo-naaganinaa is a living treaty with the Haudenosaunee, the Nishnaabeg understanding of it can give us great insight into Nishnaabeg traditions governing treaty making, and their expectations in their early interactions with settler governments. According to our prophecies, the Nishnaabeg knew a "light-skinned" race was coming to their territory.[70] They expected to have to share their territory. The expected Gdoo-naaganinaa would be taken care of so that their way of life could continue for generations to come. They expected respect for their government, their sovereignty, and their nation. They expected a relationship of peace, mutual respect and mutual benefit; and these were the same expectations the Nishnaabeg carried with them into the colonial period. Indeed, these are the expectations we carry with us into meetings with settler governments today.

Too often in contemporary times we are presented with a view of the world that renders us incapable of visioning any alternatives to our present situation and relationship with colonial governments and settler states. Biskaabiiyang compels us to return to our own knowledge systems to find answers. For Nishnaabeg peoples, Gdoo-naaganinaa does just that. It gives us an ancient template for realizing separate jurisdictions within a shared territory. It outlines the "rights" and "responsibilities" of both parties in the on-going relationship, and it clearly demonstrates that our Ancestors did not intend for our nations to be subsumed by the British Crown or the Canadian state when they negotiated those original treaties.

One does not have to give birth or breastfeed to come to understand Gdoo-naaganinaa, but those processes were critical to *my* understanding of Gdoo-naaganinaa. The process of birthing and mothering within a Nishnaabeg cultural context was the process by which I could engage in Biskaabiiyang to decolonize my understanding of treaties and treaty relationships. The seven-year cycle that spanned those initial experiences and the writing of this chapter enabled that knowledge to become Debwewin. When I cast my stone in the water by offering Edna Manitowabi tobacco to help with the safe arrival of my child into the world, I intended to reclaim birth and infant care traditions. I did not plan on learning about Nishnaabeg political culture, governance and international relations. Emergençe took care of that. If our political cultures begin at home, and our families are the microcosm for governance, then what are we currently teaching our children about leadership? Decision making? Nation building?

142 Kiera Ladner and Leanne Betasamosake Simpson, "This is an Honour Song," in Leanne Betasamosake Simpson and Kiera Ladner, eds., *This is an Honour Song: Twenty Years Since the Blockades*, Arbeiter Ring Publishing, Winnipeg, MB, 2010, 8.

143 Kiera Ladner, "From Little Things…," in Leanne Betasamosake Simpson and Kiera Ladner, eds., *This is an Honour Song: Twenty Years Since the Blockades*, Arbeiter Ring Publishing, Winnipeg, MB, 2010, 290–291.

144 Neal McLeod, *Cree Narrative Memory: From Treaties to Contemporary Times*, Purich Publisher, Saskatoon, SK, 2007, 6.

145 Neal McLeod, *Cree Narrative Memory: From Treaties to Contemporary Times*, Purich Publisher, Saskatoon, SK, 2007, 7–8

146 Neal McLeod, *Cree Narrative Memory: From Treaties to Contemporary Times*, Purich Publisher, Saskatoon, SK, 2007, 6.

147 Wendy Makoons Geniusz, *Our Knowledge is Not Primitive: Decolonizing Botanical Anishinaabe Teachings*, Syracuse University Press, Syracuse, NY, 2009, 11.

148 Doug Williams retells this part of this Creation story online at <www. storiesofthenightsky.ca/ontario.htm>, accessed June 9, 2010.

149 Doug Williams, <www.storiesofthenightsky.ca/ontario.htm>, accessed June 9, 2010.

150 A previous version of this paper was published in the *Wicazo Sa Review*, 23.2, Fall 2008: 29–42, and was republished as "Looking After Gdoo-naaganinaa: Precolonial Nishnaabeg Diplomatic and Treaty Relationships," in the forthcoming anthology by Susan A. Miller and James Riding In, eds., *Native Historians Write Back: Decolonizing American Indian History*, University of Texas Press, Lubbock, TX. In these academic contexts, I removed the initial section on breastfeeding in response to reviewer's comments, but never felt good about that. The experience of breastfeeding was the seminal turning point in my thinking on treaties. If Edna Manitowabi had not spelled out that link to me, the rest of the paper

would not have followed. Indeed, my entire thinking on treaty making would be much different.

151 James Morrison, "The Robinson Treaties of 1850: A Case Study," research study prepared for RCAP (1994), as cited in the *Final Report of the Royal Commission of Aboriginal People*, Volume 1, note 35, <www.ainc-inac.gc.ca/ch/rcap/sg/sg11_e.html#36>, accessed January 5, 2008. I confirmed this with Shirley Williams (Peterborough, ON, February 21, 2008) and she gave me the correct spelling in the double vowel system. The other word for treaty, according to both of these sources is *Bgedinige*, which means letting go.

152 Indigenous nations conceptualized governance, sovereignty, and nationalism differently than their European counterparts. For a discussion, see Patricia Monture-Angus, *Journeying Forward: Dreaming First Nations Independence*, Fernwood Publishing, Halifax, NS; and Kiera Ladner's "Women and Blackfoot Nationalism," *Journal of Canadian Studies*, 35.2 (2000): 35–60.

153 To western scientists, different species of fish gather at this location in the spring and fall to migrate and spawn. To the Nishnaabeg, these are not just "species of fish;" they are nations within their own right, with political structures unto their own. This reflects a different conceptualization of "nationalism," similar to the conceptualizations in Kiera Ladner's *Women and Blackfoot Nationalism*. To be clear, fish clans represent the Nishnaabeg people, fish nations are the actual species of fish.

154 Mnjikanming is located near Orillia, ON and has a series of ancient fish weirs reminding us of this relationship.

155 John Borrows, *Recovering Canada: The Resurgence of Indigenous Law*, University of Toronto Press, Toronto, ON, 2002, 16–20.

156 Borrows notes that there are many slightly different versions of this story in print and in our oral traditions. John Borrows, *Recovering Canada: The Resurgence of Indigenous Law*, University of Toronto Press, Toronto, ON, 2002, 19.

157 Judy DaSilva is a Traditional Knowledge Holder and environmental activist from Grassy Narrows First Nation, Grassy Narrows, ON. Interviewed by Leanne Betasamosake Simpson, March 31, 2003..

158 *Dewe'igan* is our word for drum, and it means the centre of our nations or the heartbeat. Anton Treuer, *The Assassination of Hole in the Day*, Borealis Books, St. Paul, MN, 2010, 15.

159 The last time I heard this story it was told in April 2010 by Michi Saagiig Nishnaabe big drum carrier Adrian Webb as part of our local language nest. Likely several written versions exist, but my understanding is based solely on oral versions. Steve Teekens (Nipissing First Nation), First Nations House, University of Toronto, Toronto, ON, March 2004.

160 This is a sacred story and it is not appropriate to share the entire version in this forum. What is shared is a very simplistic and short sketch and it is used here to illustrate my point.

161 Gdoo-naaganinaa is the correct spelling in the Fiero orthography eastern Ojibwe dialect. According to Alan Corbiere, Project Coordinator of Kinoomaadoog at M'Chigeeng First Nation, May 4, 2007, this treaty between the Nishnaabeg Nation and the Haudenosaunee Confederacy is called *Gdoo-naaganinaa* by the Nishnaabeg, both in the oral tradition and in historical documents written in Nishnaabemowin, and it means "Our Dish." This is the inclusive form, as opposed to the *ndoo-naaganinaa*: "our dish (but not yours)." See Victor P. Lytwyn's research into historical documents that contain the concept and also use the term *Kidonaganina*. "A Dish with One Spoon: The Shared Hunting Grounds Agreement in the Great Lakes and St. Lawrence Valley Region," *Papers of the 28th Algonquian Conference*, David H. Pentland, ed., University of Manitoba, Winnipeg, MB, 1997, 210–227.

162 To the Haudenosaunee, this treaty is known as the "Dish with One Spoon." The wampum belt for the treaty is housed in the Royal Ontario Museum in Toronto, ON.

163 According to Haudenosaunee scholar Susan Hill, "The Haudenosaunee are a confederacy comprised of five original member nations—Mohawk, Oneida, Onondaga, Cayuga and Seneca—and several 'dependent' nations, including the Tuscarora (officially the 'Sixth Nation'), Delaware, Nanticoke and Tutelo. The Haudenosaunee are also known as the Iroquois Confederacy, the Five Nations and the Six Nations." Susan Hill, "Traveling Down the River of Life Together in Peace and Friendship, Forever: Haudenosaunee Land Ethics and Treaty Agreements as the Basis for Restructuring the Relationship with the British Crown," Leanne Betasamosake Simpson, ed., *Lighting the Eighth Fire: The Liberation, Resurgence and Protection of Indigenous Nations*, Arbeiter Ring, Winnipeg, MB, 2008, 23–47.

164 For a detailed historical discussion of Kidonaganina based on archival documents from the 17th, 18th and 19th centuries, please see Victor P. Lytwyn, "A Dish with One Spoon: The Shared Hunting Grounds Agreement in the Great Lakes and St., Lawrence Valley Region," *Papers of the 28th Algonquian Conference*, David H. Pentland, ed., University of Manitoba, Winnipeg, MB, 1997, 210–227.

165 Leanne Betasamosake Simpson, *Traditional Ecological Knowledge: Insights, Issues and Implications*, Unpublished Ph.D. Dissertation, University of Manitoba, Winnipeg, MB, 1999.

166 The Dish Wampum Belt is currently housed at the Royal Ontario Museum.

167 The purpose of this paper is to focus on discussing Nishnaabe pre-colonial treaty-making processes. For discussions of the treaty from an Haudenosaunee perspective, see Barbara Gray's "The Effects of the Fur Trade on Peace: A Haudenosaunee Woman's Perspective," in *Aboriginal People and the Fur Trade: Proceedings of the 8th North American Fur Trade Conferences*, Louise Johnson, ed., Dollco Printing, Akwesasne, Mohawk Territory, 2001; and J. A. Gibson, "*Concerning the League: The Iroquois League Tradition as Dictated in Onondaga*," H. Woodbury, R. Henry and H. Webster, eds., *Algonquian and Iroquoian Linguistics Memoir 9*, 1991.

168 Barbara Gray, "The Effects of the Fur Trade on Peace: A Haudenosaunee Woman's Perspective," in *Aboriginal People and the Fur Trade: Proceedings of the 8th North American Fur Trade Conferences*, Louise Johnson, ed., Dollco Printing, Akwesasne, Mohawk Territory, 2001.

169 Susan Hill, *The Clay We Are Made of: An Examination of Haudenosaunee Land Tenure on the Grand River Territory*, Unpublished Ph.D. Dissertation, Department of Indigenous Studies, Trent University, Peterborough, ON, 2006; Susan Hill "Traveling Down the River of Life Together in Peace and Friendship, Forever: Haudenosaunee Land Ethics and Treaty Agreements as the Basis for Restructuring the Relationship with the British Crown," Leanne Betasamosake Simpson, ed., *Lighting the Eighth Fire: The Liberation, Resurgence and Protection of Indigenous Nations*, Arbeiter Ring, Winnipeg, MB, 2008, 23–47.

170 Edward Benton-Banai, *The Mishomis Book*, Indian Country Communications, Hayward. WI, 1988, 89-93.

Chapter Seven

PROTECTING THE FIRST HILL: NURTURING ENIIGAANZID IN CHILDREN

Resurgence movements need leadership. And it requires a different kind of leadership than expressed in band councils and contemporary Indigenous organizations, because many of these individuals and organizations have adopted styles of leadership that are western-based and counter to the basic values and tenets of Nishnaabeg lifeways.

When I think of leadership, I think of individuals in my life that have influenced, inspired, encouraged and brought out the very best in me. Many of these people were, or are, Elders who embody gentleness, kindness, respect, humility, and have grounded, authentic sources of power that come from working within the emergent forces of nature and the implicate order, rather than from authoritarian power. I have worked alongside these people and watched as they empowered youth to self-actualize, make mistakes, figure out solutions, grow, and become fully present creative forces in our communities by divesting of their own authority or power. In essence, they "lead by following." They teach by allowing students to direct their own learning. They are always around us, like our clans and non-human spirit beings, but they are not *directing* us.

One aspect of leadership that I have observed and heard stories about, but have rarely seen in print, is the emerging nature of leadership in Nishnaabeg governance. It is my understanding that formal governance occurred most often in the summer months, when the clans gathered together or as it was needed when issues arose. Different clans had different responsibilities, and therefore different areas of expertise. This division of responsibilities necessitated different leaders—as did the plurality of issues a family group, clan or community might face. When particular issues arose, leaders emerged according to their expertise (a combination of authentic power, knowledge, experience and personal gifts or attributes as recognized by the collective). Linda Clarkson, Vern Morrisette and Gabriel Régallet explain:

> While the clan was represented at the central fire it was not always represented by the same person. In fact, who was there was dependant [sic] upon the decision to be made. If it had to do with the assessment of the resources of the immediate territory, the clans would send their best hunters and medicine people to discuss the issue at hand. Quite simply, they were the best barometers of the resources and could make informed discussion on the subject. As well, medicine people were used to forecast the potential of the resources from their knowledge of the seasons, changes in patterns and their intimate relationship with the spirit world. If it were a decision that related to contact with another band, warriors and statesmen would be sent to discuss the matter. When we call people warriors, consider it in the context of protectors of the people not in the context of a standing army that is the reality of today.[171]

Basil Johnston also sees traditional Nishnaabeg leadership as pluralistic:

> Ogimauh [means] the foremost leader. The term is derived from *Ogindaussoowin*, which means to count or calculate. In referring to a leader, the term means he (or she) who counts a number of followers and, conversely, he (or she) who many count. Leaders did not seek followers; followers sought them. It was common for a community to have more than one leader, just as there are many flocks of geese, each with its own leader.[172]

If it was common for communities to have more than one leader, then within our political traditions we should have ways of recognizing, respecting, and reconciling different leaders within our communities. We just need to look.

When leadership is defined as simple statesmen or in terms of international politics, we are mirroring western styles of leadership rather than honouring our own traditions. Leadership within the Nishnaabeg nation and within our clans was diffused, shared, and emergent arising out of need. It ensured egalitarian social organization to a greater degree than the hierarchy that emerges when certain clans or certain individuals are placed in permanent positions of leadership and no other kinds of leaders or leadership are recognized.

Fortunately, I see this kind of traditional leadership alive and well in both urban and reserve-based Nishnaabeg communities. In my own urban community, leaders emerge and then divest themselves of that responsibility. Leaders emerge to bring about artistic and creative festivals, to start language nests, to host youth groups and women's groups, to form midwifery collectives and breastfeeding support groups, to initiate cultural immersion schools, to hold medicine camps training people to become healers. In the reserve communities I work with, I see Elders councils taking on leadership roles around the protection of land; I see individuals emerging as leaders against environmental contamination and deforestation; I see women organizing to improve the health and well-being of their children's lives, sometimes with the support of *Indian Act* administrations and sometimes without. I see a variety of leaders, sacrificing and organizing for their people based on their individual gifts and responsibilities, outside, and even in rare cases, from inside of the Indian Act system of governance. I also see traditional political leaders destabilizing that system as well. Our system of governance has not been lost; it needs attention and support, but it is not lost. Too many of us have lost the ability to *see* and recognize what needs to be done to strengthen it.

While many Nishnaabemowin speakers use the word *Ogimaa*, or in my dialect *Gimaa*, to denote leadership, Gdigaa Migizi uses another term. *Eniigaanzid* means "the one to go first," "the first to face the future," "the first to face danger," and also "the one that should be acting as protector."[173] He explained this to me as "one who leads with reluctance" and it is done out of a sense of responsibility and sacrifice, rather than desire for esteem and accolades. Eniigaanzid embodies the concepts of Aanjigone and Naakgonige. Eniigaanzid is not an authoritarian style of leadership based on unilateral decision making, coercion and hierarchy. It is a style of leadership based on humility, emergence, collectivity in decision making, sharing of the work and in action, and listening. Examples of these kinds of leaders in modern society are hard to find because they are counter to nearly all of the narratives on leadership our children are exposed to, as well as those leadership styles we mirror and model in our daily lives.

Aabawaadiziiwin

For Indigenous Peoples, our children learn about governance, power, decision making and our political cultures first and foremost in our families. The family is the microcosm for the nation. Parents model leadership. When we model coercion, hierarchy and authoritarian power we produced political leaders who embody those values. If we want to create leaders of resurgence based on a different set of values and a different conceptualization of leadership, then we had better model that to our children from the very beginning. This kind of leadership needs to be modeled to our children so they can begin to embody it from a young age. Our current education institutions have no capacity to meet this need. Aabawaadiziwin is a word that means togetherness, or the art of being together; and it means that we must practice good relationships with all living beings around us.[174] This begins in our families and with our children.

The Four Hills of Life

Nishnaabeg Elders have a series of teachings regarding the Four Stages of Life: babies and children, youth, adults, and Elders. As we walk through each stage of life, we face a series of challenges, making it difficult to climb up the hill. Many do not make it to the top.[175] For those who do make it, they walk down the other side to face the next hill of life. Sometimes this is explained as the Seven Stages of Life: the good life (abinoojiiyensag, babies), the fast life (kwezensag miinwaa gwiizensag, little girls and boys), the wandering life (oshkinaweg miinwaa oshkiniigikweg, adolescent boys and girls), the three adult stages of truth, planning and doing (ininiwag, men and miinwaa ikwewag, women), and the Elder life (Nokomis miinwaa Mishomis, Grandmother and Grandfather).[176] In the pre-colonial Nishnaabeg nation, children were highly respected *people*, valued for their insights, their humour, and their contributions to families and communities at each stage of their lives. Children were seen as Gifts, and parenting was an honour. Coming from the spirit-world at birth, children were closer to that world than their adult counterparts, and were therefore considered to have greater spiritual power—a kind of power highly respected amongst the Nishnaabeg. Adults had a lot to learn from these small teachers. Parenting strategies were developed with these core beliefs in mind, along with basic ethics regarding relationships and behaviour, while also considering the kinds of adults and communities Nishnaabeg people wanted to create and live in. Nishnaabeg families and communities were of critical importance in supporting parents in what is described as a "prolonged" attachment phase. They also had a part in gently guiding children to respect the values, core philosophies, ethics and boundaries of the society.[177] This kind of environment created highly autonomous individuals that were also community-minded. Interdependence was a core value of many precolonial Indigenous societies.[178] It also created leaders that were able to build consensus by listening to the people, leaders who were full of humility, responsibility and respect, leaders who were willing to sacrifice on a personal level for the betterment of the nation.[179] It was a kind of leadership based on shared, not absolute power, grounded in an authentic power rather than an authoritarian one; and it created communities that were profoundly *less* authoritarian, less coercive and less hierarchical than their European counterparts.[180]

Colonizers mistakenly interpreted (and continue to interpret) Nishnaabeg parenting philosophies as "a lack of parenting" because of the absence of punishment, coercion, manipulation, criticism, authoritarian power, and hierarchy. Champlain first observed, "These children are extremely spoiled, as a result of not being punished, and are of so perverse a nature that they strike their fathers and mothers, which is a sort of curse that God sends them."[181] He made similar well-known criticisms of Nishnaabeg governance and gender relations.[182] Through the lens of racism and Eurocentrism, the colonizers failed to recognize that Nishnaabeg parenting was rooted in attachment, *following* children through their stages of development, with empathy, patience, unconditional love, mutual respect, and freedom of choice.[183] These are many of the same values that are continually reflected in broader Nishnaabeg society, particularly in gender relations, diplomacy and the political culture of the pre-colonial Nishnaabeg nation.

Indigenous scholars concerned with decolonizing and Indigenous resurgence have often criticized Aboriginal leadership for a lack of commitment to these goals and adherence to the values and ethics of Indigenous political cultures.[184] In *Wasáse*, Taiaiake Alfred discusses the need for "regenerating our people so that we can support traditional government models. Regretfully, the levels of participation in social and political life, the physical fitness, and the cultural skills these models require are far beyond our weakened and dispirited people right now."[185] Resurgence is about addressing this weakened and dispirited state we find ourselves in; and one way to address this is in the way we parent our children. Nurturing children following Nishnaabeg ways produced a very different kind of family, society and nation. This is evident in the kinds of governance Indigenous Peoples engaged in, the kind of leaders our nations produced, and the kinds of political cultures we nurtured. It is my understanding that pre-colonial Nishnaabeg leadership was essentially, as Ladner writes, the Blackfoot "non-hierarchical, non-coercive and non-authoritarian."[186] Leadership was an institution that was shared amongst those with certain expertise and leaders emerged and dissolved as issues emerged and were resolved. It was the responsibility of leaders not to assert their will onto the people, but to co-operatively generate consensus.[187] Leadership skills were passed down to younger generations through the Clan responsible for this task.[188] Individuals led on the basis of their Gifts, and their commitment to their people. Relationships were of the utmost importance. "Powerful" leaders adhered to the Kokum Dibaajimowinan and influenced the people in a non-authoritarian fashion.

Kokum Dibaajimowinan

Recall the Seven Grandfather Teachings from Chapter Four. These teachings include: Aakde'ewin, the art of having courage; Debwewin, the art of truth or sincerity; Mnaadendiwin, the art of having respect; Zaagidewin, the art of love or loving; Gwekwaadiziwin, the art of being honest; Nbwaakawin, the art of wisdom; and Dbadendiziwin, the art of humility. When I asked Gdigaa Migizi what our Michi Saagiig Nishnaabeg Elders called the Seven Grandfather Teachings in our territory, he immediately answered, "Kokum Dibaajimowinan," *Grandmother* teachings.[189]

One fall afternoon I asked him to share with me his understanding of these words. We began with Aakde'ewin,[190] which is commonly translated as "courage" or the "art of being brave." Gdigaa Migizi explained that this means "strong hearted," not in a physical sense, but in relation to Debwewin. Aakde'yin might be used to describe the weakest person physically, but this kind of strength comes from knowing who one is, a grounding in self-knowledge. So Aakde'yin might describe the one that is given strength from family, stories, teachings. Because of this self-knowledge, one who has Aakde'yin is without fear of a foe or the unknown, because he or she is confident in who he or she is and where he or she is going. Of course, this "confidence" is exercised within the context of tremendous humility.

In speaking to Debwewin, the art of truth, or the "sound of the heart," Gdigaa Migizi stressed speaking from the heart, and that his understanding of Debwewin was not physical, but involved the idea that "being a good person was being a person whose word you could trust." He explained that Kokum Dibaajimowinan were often explained by describing a specific attribute in a person; that is, the teachings were personalized. So the old people would describe the teachings using someone who embodied the teachings as an example.

Mnaadendiwin is often translated as "respect" or the "art of respect," but Gdigaa Migizi explained that this means that we are to deeply cherish each other. We are to work towards seeing each other and cherishing each other for who we are, and in doing so, we become one. We become a family of deeply cherished individuals of one mind. This teaching flows into Aanjigone in that we are to be very slow to judge one another, very careful with our words and actions to not bring those negative attributes back onto ourselves and our families.

For Zaagidewin, commonly translated as "love," Gdigaa Migizi spoke of an unconditional love, similar to the qualities expressed in Gzhwe. He spoke of one bearing their soul and heart nakedly, expressing a complete vulnerability, reminding me of a newborn baby. When one comes to another bearing his or her soul, completely trusting that the other person will be non-judgmental, caring and gentle, he or she comes expecting acceptance, gentleness, kindness and nurturing. In the context of Kokum Dibaajimowinan, this is what is meant by "love."

Gwekwaadiziwin is often used to describe one that lives a "straight" life, an honest life or the "art of being honest." Gdigaa Migizi instead used the term Kaazhaadizi and explained it as a person that is all of the above—a good person with peace of mind and both feet on the ground. A person with Kaazhaadizi embodies love, is totally giving, and openly accepts another person. Shirley Williams understood this word in a similar way, and defined it as "to be kind." [191]

One way that gentleness, kindness and humility are expressed in our intellectual pursuits is through the concept of Nbwaakawin, [192] commonly translated as knowledge. According to Shirley Williams, it means "the art of kindness in knowledge." Shirley explained to me that Nbwaakawin means to put others before one's own self. In other words, you can think about yourself after you have thought about others, so that even though you might have knowledge or know about a particular concept, you cannot always show what you know. In a sense, Nbwaakawin keeps ego in check (which is the third level of consciousness in Nishnaabeg thought). This concept refers to the highest form of wisdom and it cautions people to be careful with that wisdom and use it in an appropriate way. If one follows Nbwaakawin, one will know how to handle this kind of wisdom and also remain in a humble state. [193] This is performed by Elders in Nishnaabeg communities and is one of the concepts that often confuses western experts. The expression of tremendous humility around knowledge and knowing is something that authentic Elders do constantly. This concept is an important reminder for leaders, parents and teachers of all kinds.

Dbadendiziwin [194] is the art of being humble or humility, to never look upon oneself as being better than anyone else. It also means to look after or maintain oneself. To me, this means that in order to keep that ego in check, we have to look after our spiritual, emotional, physical and intellectual selves in order to maintain balance.

As a Nishnaabeg mother, I see it as a core responsibility of mine to ensure my children are grounded in Nishnaabeg values and ethics as best I can. This includes Kokum Dibaajimowinan, while also having the skills to critically engage the colonial. As a Nishnaabeg mother, I understand that I have a responsibility to decolonize my own mothering skills to create space within my family for Nishnaabeg philosophies to flourish. I am not suggesting we blindly adopt all pre-colonial Indigenous parenting techniques.[195] There was a great diversity amongst Indigenous Peoples in the kinds of childrearing practices they employed,[196] and not all of the pre-colonial techniques are acceptable or desirable in contemporary times. Our children live in a very different world than their pre-colonial counterparts, and they have to be able to live and function in (at least) two worlds, so complete immersion into pre-colonial parenting traditions is not only impossible, but it is also not desirable. Further, they need to be able to think and act critically, anti-colonially and honourably from an Indigenous perspective. They are the ones that will carry on our responsibility in building resurgence.

Decolonizing parenting techniques means figuring out the kinds of citizens we want to create, the kinds of communities we want to live in, and the kinds of leaders we want to create, then tailoring our parenting and our schooling to meet the needs of our nations. Residential schools, the colonial child welfare system, dominant interpretations of Christianity and mandatory colonial schooling have not allowed for our parenting styles to evolve to meet the needs of modern Indigenous communities; similarly, mainstream parenting styles are not enough to create leaders and citizens grounded in Indigenous cultural and political traditions that are able to confront and lead people through the many facets of colonialism. If we are truly interested in decolonizing, then we must critically evaluate how we are parenting and educating the next generation because it is one of the few areas of our lives we can assert a certain degree of control and it is critical to the decolonizing project. We must rethink how our great leaders of the past were made.

Leading by Following: The Seven Stages of Life

Parents are a child's first and often most profound experience with leadership. For the Nishnaabeg, the first relationships a child experiences are critically important because they provide the model for all other relationships to follow. It is a common Nishnaabeg belief that if you are an authoritarian parent, you will create adults and leaders who are also authoritarian. Authoritarian parents create adults whose leadership skills revolve around absolute power.

A few years ago at Trent University's Annual Elder and Traditional People's gathering, I heard traditional teacher Sylvia Maracle talk about her understanding of the Seven Stages of Life.[197] She went through each stage of life, thoroughly inverting settler society's view of children as empty vessels in need of control, instruction, boundaries and teaching. From her perspective, children have it right already; it is the adults that need to learn. This model is also profoundly non-hierarchical, as the Seven Stages of Life are presented as a circle.

In her discussion of the first stage, infancy, she talked about how infants teach their parents and extended family about love, the kind of love that is unconditional, based on sacrifice and putting the needs of others before oneself. Toddlers teach the importance of safe environments as they busily explore and learn about their environment. Children teach us, often humorously. about truth, unaware of the culturally constructed norms around the kinds of information shared publicly and the kinds not. Our youth remind us of teachings around rejection and establishing one's own sense of self, important teachings that give way to young adults who are responsible for the "work of the nation." Parents are firmly in the "planting stage" of life, sowing the seeds for the next generation, and nurturing those seedlings to adulthood. The primary responsibility of parents is that of provider; so during this life phase, contributions to the wider community and nation are kept to a minimum. This "paid parental leave," associated in modern times with the highly "civilized" states of the world, was a cornerstone of pre-colonial Nishnaabeg parenting styles because Nishnaabeg people recognized that the *quality* of the parent-child relationship was the foundation of non-authoritarian parenting.

In the late 1990s, I was involved in a repatriation project that took me to the Smithsonian Institute in Washington, DC. I was looking at a "collection" of Gashkibidaaganag[198] with Mark Thompson-ba, a Nishnaabeg medicine person from Manitoba.[199] He explained to me the meaning that the beadwork on each bag is a form of language that communicated the particular medical and healing skills of the owner. Each bag however, had a section that was completely blank, absent of beadwork. When I asked Mark what that meant, he explained that this was the period of time when the owner of the bag stopped learning about medicinal plants because they were busy raising their children. Nishnaabeg people saw their parental responsibilities as paramount. They recognized that children require a lot of time, and that healthy relationships take time to foster, develop and maintain. Nishnaabeg parents have been taking parental leave for thousands and thousands of years.

The other important concept in our teachings regarding the Seven Stages of Life is the responsibilities of extended family in nurturing children. Everyone is both a teacher and a learner in this model; each individual both teaches and learns different things at different stages in their lives. Grandparents were responsible for teaching their grandchildren, often through the use of personal and traditional stories, as well as life's lessons. Community Elders taught children spiritual lessons.[200] The sharing of responsibilities around children takes the pressure for complete childrearing off the parents and is a fundamental requirement for parenting that is non-authoritarian in nature.

Protecting the First Hills of Life

In terms of resurgence, we need to make sure more of our babies, children and youth are making it to the top of their hills, that they are healthy and full of life once they get there, that they have made it through their struggles using Nishnaabeg ways of being, and that they have cared for others on the way.

Nengaajgchigewin in Parenting

Nengaajgchigewin means the art of doing something gentle, to be gentle on something.[201] This permeates Nishnaabeg parenting practices, especially for infants with extended nursing, strong attachment to the mother, and immediate response to infant's cries. Infants bring with them a tremendous amount of unconditional love from the Spirit

World. In following this philosophy, it is our responsibility to respond to them with that same unconditional love. Recognizing that they are people with needs, it is the parent's responsibility to figure what those needs are and how to respond to them. This is in sharp contrast to settler style parenting strategies, centred around detachment—placing infants alone in cribs for long periods of time, scheduled bottle feeding, and "crying it out." These strategies are an avoidance of parental responsibilities justified by attempting to create infants that can self-soothe and obtain a level of self-sufficiency (i.e. require no parental effort at night).[202] Strong attachment parenting followed children often as long as they needed it (with extended nursing and communal sleeping areas) because there was a fundamental belief that children only asked for things as long as they needed them. Children were continually given the benefit of the doubt. They were never far from parents, so parents were always there to calm any fears. Some of these practices extended into the colonial period and to present day. My Grandmother, who has very few happy childhood memories, recalls that sleeping in her Grandparents' bedroom along the shore of Pimaadashkodeyong was the time in her life she felt the most safe.

Culturally based Nishnaabe parenting styles assumed that infants were utterly dependent upon their parents and they worked hard to meet those needs. During my first pregnancy, an Elder directed my partner and I to construct a Tikanagan, a traditional baby carrier.[203] She told us a traditional story about how the Tikanagan came to the Nishnaabeg people. In short, a young Nishnaabekwe new mother was having trouble living up to her responsibilities to her family because her baby would cry whenever she put her down. One day, exhausted and frustrated, she came upon a Haudenosaunee woman in the bush, with her baby snuggled into a Tikanagan. The young Nishnaabekwe carefully observed the moss bag and the carrying apparatus and went home that night to construct one of her own. She was then able to wrap her baby and take her everywhere with her, simultaneously calming the baby and completing her other responsibilities to her family. Our Tikanagan hangs in our home now that our children have out grown it, and it serves as a constant reminder of traditional Nishnaabeg parenting values: interdependence, non-interference, teaching by modeling, learning by doing. It also reminds us of the importance of co-operation, generosity, sharing, non-competitiveness, harmony and respect for life in Nishnaabeg society.

Zhinoomoowin: Modeling and Learning by Doing

Zhinoomoowin is the art of showing someone something, to act, or to show how it is done, in other words modeling desirable behaviours for children to mimic.[204] In Nishnaabeg philosophies regarding education and knowledge, Zhinoomoowin is a very important way of teaching children—more important than telling or directing. Good relations provide the context for everything from learning to governing and interacting with other nations. Great lengths went into preserving, maintaining and nurturing relationships personally, ceremonially and collectively. This is true also for parenting. The relationship between the parent and child was extremely important and parents were taught that the primary nurturing relationship should be positive, supportive, and absent of fear.[205] This is part of the reason that there was an absence of punishment in traditional Nishnaabeg society. Former Crown attorney Rupert Ross recounts this experience in his book, *Returning to the Teachings*: "At one point I asked what the community used to do in traditional times, before the courts came, to those who misbehaved. An old lady answered immediately. Through an interpreter she said, "We didn't do anything *to* them. We counseled them instead."[206] There was a strong commitment to learning and healing in the restorative justice system of the Nishnaabeg and this extended into family relations. Punishment was frowned upon because it was seen as violent, interfering, and authoritarian.[207] But pre-colonial Nishnaabeg also recognized that punishment was not a good tool for teaching in the long term. Fear of punishment may cause children to avoid undesirable behaviours in the short term, but in the long run, it teaches them it is all right to exert violence onto a smaller or weaker individual—something abhorred in the Nishnaabe worldview. Counseling, healing and taking responsibility for one's actions, on the other hand, eventually guide children into avoiding undesirable behaviours not out of fear, but out a sense of right and wrong. The belief that children deserve to be treated with dignity, respect, understanding and compassion, just like any adult, simply meant that manipulation, excessive praise, punishment, rewards, withholding of privileges, criticism, and threats were out of the question as parenting strategies.

The same is true for criticism. I have never heard a legitimate Nishnaabeg Elder ever offer anything remotely resembling criticism, and sometimes members of my generation mistakenly interpret this as complacency.[208] In my experience, nothing could be further from the truth. The older ones hang onto their traditional values tightly, and rather than criticizing others, they are committed to offering alternatives and solutions. They are committed to Aanjigone and to processing emotions in a healthy way.[209] Criticism and anger are immediately communicated by silence. After a period of conservative withdrawal, people engage in open discussion, healing and solution building.

Modeling is central to Nishnaabeg beliefs around parenting. Parents and extended family members teach by modeling, a "do as I do" philosophy rather than a "do as I say" mentality.[210] There is a strong belief that if children are treated harshly, they will treat other harshly. If children are subjected to authoritarian parenting styles, they will in turn be authoritarian leaders. If paternalistic violence surrounds a child, she will behave in paternalistic and violent ways when she is an adult. Modeling, like other tenets of Nishnaabeg parenting, takes time to work, but in the long term has proven to be highly effective.

Aanjigone in Parenting

The concept of non-interference described earlier in this book as Aanjigone was significant in parenting. The grammatical structure of our language was founded on the premise of non-interference, making it difficult to express gossip and hearsay. Combined with our value system, people recognized they only had a right to their own experiences. They did not offer advice unless it was asked for directly. And meddling into another's affairs, under the guise of friendship or parental responsibility, was not tolerated. Nishnaabeg concepts of trust also reflect non-interference with the absence of a universal truth in exchange for a plurality of truths.[211]

Non-interference encourages children to have control over their lives and to make decisions. This is much different from the contemporary settler parenting strategy of allowing children to make choices only when they don't matter (would you like to wear your red pajamas or your blue ones?). Both of my children immediately detected the manipulative non-authentic nature of this "choice" and of course chose to sleep naked, or wear all of their pajamas to bed.

Non-interference can only work in a system where children are highly connected and attached to their parents and extended family, where the culture is inherently child-friendly. It needs to be where the culture and environment are set up so that children integrate into every part of daily life and that "good choices" are easy to make (and in the best interest of the child). Raising children with a commitment to traditional parenting styles requires a tremendous amount of time and commitment, since the quality of the relationship between the parent and the child is the base for all of life's learning. Allowing children to have freedom of choice in a detached, individualistic, adult environment would of course put children in danger; and this is the misunderstanding that settler societies continue to make in reference to Indigenous parenting philosophies. Freedom of choice is just one facet of a philosophy designed to create honourable, responsible, healthy adults.

It is my understanding that older members of the family would intervene if a child's choice was going to cause great harm to herself or to others. But in reality, this is a rare occurrence. Most parental interference is over the small stuff. The role of the parent is to love, guide and support, not to control. We allow children to make mistakes, supporting them in finding solutions to their problems.

Giving children freedom of choice has historically been treated as an abdication of parental responsibility, a sign of a lack of care and in short, an unfit parenting practice by colonial authorities, including the legal system and child and family services.[212] But it is Dr. Clare Brant's view that "children raised by non-interfering parents become enormously loyal to them and to the entire extended family. They have, after all, enjoyed only pleasurable experiences with them, free of complaint, criticism, advice or coercion."[213] Children were taught to respect boundaries through ritual, protocol, and storytelling. There are several examples in Nishnaabeg oral literature of stories designed to illicit responsible behaviour in children.[214] The enforcement of those boundaries was deliberately external to the family and the community, thus protecting the safety and security of primary nurturing relationship. Grandparents readily shared personal and traditional stories with younger family members as a mechanism for gently guiding children into behaving in an appropriate manner. Children were taken to ceremonies from the time they were infants and understood the rituals and rhythms of daily life.[215] Strong positive, nurturing connections between the child and his or her family brought out a strong desire to respect those individuals and relationships, not out of fear of punishment, but out of love, honour and genuine respect.

Parenting in a culture that requires a high level of attachment, indulgence and protection is very taxing, which is why extended family's support is so critical. The support of extended family allows mothers "breaks" from parenting in order to preserve the loving nature of their relationships with their children and prevent any one relationship from becoming "too frightening for the child."[216] The "conservative withdrawal" ethic—the idea that one retreats into one's own self when one's emotions are running high—also promotes a safe environment for women and children. Modeling this "retreat" behaviour taught Nishnaabeg children the importance of being responsible with one's own emotions, while reinforcing "healthy" ways of dealing with strong emotion. Mechanisms for dealing with anger, such as Sharing Circles and shared decision making, could occur only after emotional restraint had been regained, and this precluded hostile behaviour towards others. These tenets of traditional society ensured that gender violence and violence towards children were rare occurrences with decisive consequences and that the expression of authoritarian power was categorically less than in European society.[217]

Nurturing Leaders for Resurgence

As a parent, I continue to try to put many of these values into practice in my daily interactions with my children. It is not easy. It is not the way I was raised. I am certainly more controlling than I mean to be; and I have at times, often in desperation and suffering from exhaustion, been coercive, manipulative and authoritarian. Nishnaabeg parenting is not a parenting style that is even remotely supported by settler society, and in contemporary times, few of us have the support of extended families and healthy communities to assist us. The legacy of the child welfare system and residential schools means that I have no role models in my family or my community for what I am trying to accomplish. Contemporary Nishnaabeg parents do not have many of the requirements for this kind of parenting at their disposal—the support of extended family committed to decolonizing their interactions with children and paid long-term parental leave. We do not necessarily live in communities that are able to gently convey a cohesive set of values to our children. However, many facets of this parenting philosophy are "do-able" in a modern context for many Nishnaabeg families, and I believe they are vital to passing on a legacy of responsibility, hope and love to the next generation. Just as stories stitch together our nation, children are the glue that holds our families together. It is my hope that we begin to honour them as such.[218]

---

171 Linda Clarkson, Vern Morrisette and Gabriel Régallet, *Our Responsibility to the Seventh Generation: Indigenous Peoples and Sustainable Development*, International Institute for Sustainable Development, Winnipeg, MB, 1992, 17.

172 Basil Johnston, *The Manitous: The Spiritual World of the Ojibway*, Key Porter Books, Toronto, ON, 1996, 244. John Borrows noted in previous drafts of this book that this interpretation of the word was consistent with what he had been taught as a young person.

173 Vanessa Watts, *Towards Anishinaabe Governance and Accountability: Reawakening our Relationships and Sacred Bimaadiziwin*, unpublished MA thesis, Indigenous Governance Program, University of Victoria, Victoria, BC, 2004, 89, <web.uvic.ca /igov/research/pdfs/Vanessa%20Watts%20-%20Thesis.pdf>, accessed September 20, 2010. I confirmed this with Doug Williams, Waawshkigaamagki (Curve Lake First Nation), July 15, 2010.

174 This was explained by Elder Fred Kelly (Onigaming First Nation) to Vanessa Watts, *Towards Anishnaabe Governance and Accountability: Reawakening our Relationships and Sacred Bimaadiziwin*, unpublished MA Thesis, Indigenous Governance Programs, University of Victoria, Victoria, BC, 2004, <web.uvic.ca/igov/ research/pdfs/Vanessa%20Watts%20-%20Thesis.pdf>, accessed September 20, 2010. It means "togetherness," in the sense that one must practice good relationships

and fulfill their responsibilities to themselves, their families, community, clan, nation and the natural world.

175 Basil Johnston, *Ojibway Heritage: The Ceremonies, Rituals, Songs, Dances, Prayers and Legends of the Ojibway*, McClelland Stewart, Toronto, ON, 1976, 109–119; Thomas Peacock and Marlene Wisuri, *The Four Hills of Life: Ojibwe Wisdom*, Afton Historical Society Press, Afton, MN, 2006.

176 Edna Manitowabi, Stoney Lake, ON, December 14, 2010; Lillian Pitawanakwat, <www.fourdirectionsteachings.com>, accessed September 12, 2010; Thomas Peacock and Marlene Wisuri, *The Four Hills of Life: Ojibwe Wisdom*, Afton Historical Society Press, Afton, MN, 2006.

177 Clare Brant and P.G.R Patterson, "Native Child Rearing Practices and Their Role in Mental Health," *A Collection of Chapters, Lectures, Workshops and Thoughts*, published by Ann Brant, 1997, 99–118.

178 Clare Brant and P.G.R Patterson, "Native Child Rearing Practices and Their Role in Mental Health," *A Collection of Chapters, Lectures, Workshops and Thoughts*, published by Ann Brant, 1997, 99–118.

179 For a broader discussion of pre-colonial Indigenous leadership, see Volume 2, Chapter 3 of the Final Report of the Royal Commission on Aboriginal Peoples, available online at <www.ainc-inac.gc.ca/ch/rcap/sg/sh14_e.htm>.

180 Kiera Ladner, "Governing Within an Ecological Context: Creating an AlterNative Understanding of Blackfoot Governance," *Studies in Political Economy* 70, Spring 2003: 125–152; Taiaiake Alfred, *Wasáse: Indigenous Pathways of Action and Freedom*, Broadview Press, Peterborough, ON, 2005; Andrea Smith, *Conquest: Sexual Violence and American Indian Genocide*, South End Press, Cambridge, MA, 2005.

181 Edward G Bourne, ed., *Algonquins, Huron and Iroquois, Champlain Explores America 1603–1616*, Brookhouse Press, Dartmouth, NS, 189.

182 Edward G Bourne, ed., *Algonquins, Huron and Iroquois, Champlain Explores America 1603–1616*, Brookhouse Press, Dartmouth, NS,.

183 Rupert Ross, *Dancing with a Ghost: Exploring Indian Reality*, Reed Books Canada, Markham, ON, 1992, 11–38, 116–125.

184 Taiaiake Alfred, *Wasáse: Indigenous Pathways of Action and Freedom*, Broadview Press, Peterborough, ON, 2005. See also Dale Turner's discussion of this in *This is Not a Peace Pipe: Towards a Critical Indigenous Philosophy*, University of Toronto Press, Toronto, ON, 2006, 107–108.

185 Taiaiake Alfred, *Wasáse: Indigenous Pathways of Action and Freedom*, Broadview Press, Peterborough, ON, 2005, 32.

186 Kiera Ladner, "Governing Within an Ecological Context: Creating an AlterNative Understanding of Blackfoot Governance," *Studies in Political Economy* 70, Spring 2003, 125–152.

187 Respected spiritual leader of the Nishnaabeg people, Peter O'Chiese, explains Nishnaabeg style consensus as the Seven Clans coming to an eighth

understanding: "Seven perspectives blended, seven perspectives working in harmony together to truly define the problem, truly define the action that is needed makes for an eighth understanding. It's a tough lesson that we don't know all the answers, we don't know all the problems. We really own only one-seventh of the understanding of it and we only know one-seventh of what to do about it. We need each other in harmony to know how to do things ... This process that we had was 100 per cent ownership of the problem," Mark Douglas recalling the teaching of Peter O'Chiese as quoted in the *Final Report of the Royal Commission on Aboriginal Peoples, Volume 3, Chapter 2*, available online at <www.ainc-inac.gc.ca/ch/rcap/sg/sh14_e.htm>.

188 See Edward Benton-Banai, *The Mishomis Book,* Indian Country Communications, Hayward, WI, 1988, 75–80.

189 Doug Williams, Peterborough, ON, October 27, 2010.

190 Aakde'ewin is the art of being brave, Aakde'yin is when you are brave or strong. Shirley Williams, Peterborough, ON, December 18, 2010.

191 Shirley Williams, Peterborough, ON, October 27, 2010.

192 Doug Williams was unfamiliar with this word, and would use Gikendaasawin for knowledge. Peterborough ON, October 27, 2010.

193 Shirley Williams, Peterborough, ON, September 19, 2010.

194 Vanessa Watts, *Towards Anishinaabe Governance and Accountability: Reawakening our Relationships and Sacred Bimaadiziwin,* unpublished MA thesis, Indigenous Governance Program, University of Victoria, Victoria, BC, 2004, 89, <web.uvic.ca/igov/research/pdfs/Vanessa%20Watts%20-%20Thesis.pdf>, accessed September 20, 2010. Vanessa indicated to me she learned the Seven Sacred Gift Teachings from Shirley Williams, personal communication, November 15, 2010. Doug Williams explained Nishnaabeg conceptualizations of humility to me, Peterborough, ON, October 27, 2010.

195 It is also somewhat difficult to reconstruct pre-colonial Indigenous parenting techniques. The anthropological record and the record of early explorers and settlers are all wrought with Euro-centrism, but viewed if through an Indigenous lens can reveal core concepts. Several Nishnaabeg Elders have also informed my views, including Edna Manitowabi and Robin Greene-ba.

196 Clare Brant and P.G.R Patterson, "Native Child Rearing Practices and Their Role in Mental Health," *A Collection of Chapters, Lectures, Workshops and Thoughts,* published by Ann Brant, 1997, 99–118.

197 Sylvia Maracle, *The Seven Stages of Life,* Elders' Conference, Trent University, Peterborough, ON, February 15, 2004.

198 Bandolier Bags.

199 Mark Thompson-ba was from Sagkeeng First Nation on the east side of Lake Winnipeg.

200 Teaching was not didactic, but accomplished through storytelling, ceremony, experiential learning, reflection, and modeling.

201 I explained the concept of attachment parenting in English to Shirley Williams and she said that this was encompassed in Nengaajgchigewin. Peterborough, ON, September 20, 2010.

202 See attachment theory and contemporary attachment parenting books such as William and Martha Sears' *Attachment Parenting: A Commonsense Guide to Understanding and Nurturing Your Baby*, Little, Brown and Company Publishing, New York, 2001; Katie Allison Granju with Betsy Kennedy, *Attachment Parenting: Instinctive Care for your Baby and Young Child*, Pocket Books, NY, 1999.

203 Cradleboard.

204 Similarly, Zhiinoomaagewin is the art of showing, to show something, to point at something. Shirley Williams, Peterborough ON, September 20, 2010.

205 Clare Brant and P.G.R Patterson, "Native Child Rearing Practices and Their Role in Mental Health," *A Collection of Chapters, Lectures, Workshops and Thoughts*, published by Ann Brant, 1997, 99–118.

206 Rupert Ross, *Returning to the Teachings: Exploring Aboriginal Justice*, Penguin Books, Toronto, ON, 1996, 5.

207 Because of the ethics of non-interference discussed later in this paper, children experienced the natural consequences of their actions. It is my current understanding that traditional stories had punitive elements in them as a means of externalizing punishment from the community and family while also encouraging children to behave in a responsible manner.

208 This is most definitely a result of our colonial upbringings. Nishnaabeg people have always been stereotyped as docile, lazy, and permissive by colonizers who hated the gentleness of our ways.

209 It is my understanding that emotional restraint in this context does not mean one is to suppress one's emotions, but deal with them in a responsible way that does not endanger the peace of others. Thus, people were encouraged to retreat from the social situation until their emotions were under control, followed by sharing and talking.

210 Clare Brant and P.G.R Patterson, "Native Child Rearing Practices and Their Role in Mental Health," *A Collection of Chapters, Lectures, Workshops and Thoughts*, published by Ann Brant, 1997, 99–118.

211 This is not the same as a plurality of truths in a post-modern context. While everyone was entitled to their own perspective and truths, perspectives that violated the fundamental principles and values of Nishnaabeg society were not respected. Murray Sinclair, "Aboriginal Peoples and Euro-Canadians: Two World Views," in John H. Hylton, ed., *Aboriginal Self-Government in Canada: Current Trends and Issues*, Purich Publishing, Saskatoon, SK, 1994, 19.

212 Rupert Ross, *Returning to the Teachings: Exploring Aboriginal Justice*, Penguin Books, Toronto, ON, 1996, 19.

213 Rupert Ross, *Returning to the Teachings: Exploring Aboriginal Justice*, Penguin Books, Toronto, ON, 1996, 19.

214 For example, see Edward Benton-Banai, *The Mishomis Book*, Indian Country Communications, Hayward, WI, 1988.

215 These values were reinforced at puberty with girls completing the Berry Fast for girls and boys, a Vision Quest.

216 Clare Brant and P.G.R Patterson, "Native Child Rearing Practices and Their Role in Mental Health," *A Collection of Chapters, Lectures, Workshops and Thoughts*, published by Ann Brant, 1997, 99–118.

217 Andrea Smith, *Conquest: Sexual Violence and American Indian Genocide*, South End Press, Cambridge, MA, 2005, 18–23.

218 The idea that children are the glue that holds our families and communities together was a teaching Edna Manitowabi shared with me. Stoney Lake, ON, December 14, 2010.

Chapter Eight

SHI-KIIN: NEW WORLDS

Over a decade ago I was teaching a class with Nishnaabeg Elder Robin Green-ba and a scientist at the Centre for Indigenous Environmental Resources in Winnipeg. Our class was discussing what is meant by the term "sustainable development." The scientist was explaining that it means meeting the needs (and wants) of humans without compromising the needs (and wants) of future generations. In other words, developing only to the point where that development starts to impinge on future generations. I asked Robin if there was a similar concept in Nishnaabeg thought. He thought for a moment and then answered, "No there isn't." He told the class that sustainable development thinking is backwards, that we should be doing the opposite. He explained that what makes sense from a Nishnaabeg perspective is that humans should be taking as little as possible, giving up as much as possible to promote sustainability and promote mino bimaadiziwin in the coming generations. He felt that we should be as gentle as possible with our Mother, and that we should be taking the bare minimum to ensure our survival. He talked about how we need to manage ourselves so that *life can promote more life.*

In the middle of his book X *Marks: Native Signatures of Assent,* Scott Lyons, a Nishnaabe/Dakota scholar from Minnesota, embarked on a project to see if he could find a word for "culture" in Nishnaabemowin. When I came across this section is his book, my immediate reaction was, of course not. Of course we don't have a word for culture because our "culture" was and is a series of interrelated processes that engage our full beings and require our full presence. After some searching and some consultation with Elders, Lyons came up with a roster of words and expressions including izhitwaa, nitaa, inaadizi, gaaminigoowisieng, and gaaenakowinid, that he interprets to respond to a single "overarching concern: the desire to produce more life."[219] This is consistent with Winona LaDuke's interpretation of mino bimaadiziwin as "continuous rebirth."[220] It resonated with everything I had been taught by Elders—that the goal is to promote life and to live it rather than just talk about. Lyons starts by discussing *izhitwaa*, which he signifies as "having a certain custom or practicing a certain ceremony," breaking the word down to its component parts: "twaa" denotes the sound of deep respect, reverence; and "izhi" means doing something meaningful in a certain way to produce a certain outcome. Words derived from izhitwaa include descriptors of actions of both people, animals and other components of nature. *Izhiwebezi* means to behave in a certain and expected manner, while izhitigweyaa means to flow river-like to a specific place.[221]

The second word Lyons explores is *nitaa*, which addresses the "nurturing sense of culture" and means tending to grow, to be good or skilled at something, knowing how to do it, and doing it frequently. This word is used when speaking about all aspects of creation, including humans, animals and physical components and processes of the land. *Nitaawigi* means raising a child; *nitaawigitoon* means growing a crop; nitaawe means speaking or seeing well; *nitaage* means to mourn or kill game. According to Lyons, nitaa brings about a sense of doing things to bring about more life.[222]

The third word Lyons breaks down is *inaadizi*, which means living with a particular character.[223] *Inaadiziwin* means "way of life," and its root inaadizi can signify both a utility (*inaabadizi* means to be useful or employed), while also signifying a practical reality that includes the spiritual world (inaabam suggests seeing someone in a dream). Lyons sees this as "utility linked to vision," as if one can see a proper course of action and become useful through living this way of life.[224] He continues "...there is also a judicial connotation here, as *inaakonan* refers to deciding something formally and *inaakonige* means making a judgment. Our word for law is *inaakonigwein*. Seeing, using, being useful, judging, deciding all of these acts inform inaadiziwin, suggesting that our 'way of life' is defined by certain values, namely things like utility, and clear sighted judgment, and visionary decision making."[225]

When consulting with Elder George Goggleye of Leech Lake, Lyons was given two more words to consider: gaaminigoowisieng, "that which was given to use;" and gaaenakowinid, "that which was given to the Anishinaabeg to live by."[226] Putting these concepts together, Lyon's explains:

> As rivers flow and birds fly, practicing religious ceremonies and other customs (*izhitwaa*) produces an intended result: more life. Behaving skillfully (*nitaa*) leads to more life as well, as evidenced by the proliferation of happy children and healthy crops. Living in a certain way (*inaadizi*) allows a community to see, use, decide and make clear judgments, all values guiding the making of more life. These ways of living were given to us [in a loving way] (*gaaminigoowisieng, gaaenakowinid*) by Someone or maybe Something, who wanted us to survive, thrive, and thereby produce more life. But perhaps the clearer indication of this general goal is another phrase commonly used to describe Ojibwe culture, *anishinaabe bimaadizi*, "living as Indian." *Bimaadizi* is used to describe the general state of someone being alive, and it possesses connotations of movement that can be understood in a physical sense. Consider the congnates: *bimaashi* means to be blown along, *bimaadagaa* to swim effortlessly as if to be carried by the current, *bimaada'e* to skate, and *bimaawadaaso*, to move along in a group like a school of fish. The flowing sense of living in rhythm with others, of going along with the ebb and flow of nature...[227]

Biiskaabiyaang, Naakgonige, Aanjigone and Debwewin produced and continue to produce more life. Colonialism has only created a loss of life in terms of extinct and endangered species of animals and plants, and a drastic and traumatic decline in the quality of life for the fraction of Nishnaabeg that survived the original conquest. Zhaaganashiiyaadizi destroys Nishnaabeg presence, and this is counter to mino bimaadiziwin. Resurgence movements then, must be movements to create more life, propel life, nurture life, motion, presence and emergence.

Stone's Throw

If the over-reaching goal of resurgence is to produce more life and to re-create the conditions for living as Nishnaabeg peoples following our own inherent processes and expressions of life, then our interventions into colonialism must be consistent with these core values of continuous rebirth, motion, presence and emergence. Emergence becomes of vital importance here, because within Nishnaabeg thinking around mobilization, small things are important and can have major influences over the course of time. Whether we are speaking about muskrat's paw of dirt from which this world was created, or the young person's dream that set our nation on our collective migration, desired outcomes are heavily influenced by the processes we engage in, our relationships, and how we live in this world.

This idea that living in the right way as individuals sets in motion influences and impacts that are impossible to predict is reflected in much Indigenous thinking around sovereignty. Haudenosaunee legal scholar Patricia Monture has written that self-determination and sovereignty begin at home.[228] It begins with how we treat ourselves and our family members — how we make decisions that honour the voices of all of our family members; how we respect individual autonomy and sovereignty; how we relate to human and non-human entities in a manner that embodies respect, responsibility, reciprocity and renewal. These relations then spiral outward to our communities and our nations. They extend into the network of relations in the implicate order and set up cycles of non-violence for the generations yet to come. This teaching is often visualized as a spiral, starting with the individual and radiating upwards and outwards with the circles gradually becoming larger. But according to our teachings, the spiral radiates in all seven directions — inward, outward in the four cardinal directions, upwards, downwards and through time. Resurgence works the same way. As resurgence is collectivized, it moves from being an individual act, vision or commitment, to one that functions on the level of a family. It then moves to a group of families, then a portion of a community, then a community, and so on. To me, the concept of collectivizing is encompassed in the term Nkweshkgdaadiwin, the art of meeting together.[229]

Métis Elder Maria Campbell explained this teaching to me in terms of resistance and resurgence.[230] She told me that acts of resistance are like throwing a stone into water. The stone makes its initial impact in the water, displacing it and eventually sinking to the bottom. There is the original splash the act of resistance makes, and the stone (or the act) sinks to the bottom, resting in place and time. But there are also more subtle waves of disruption that ripple or echo out from where the stone impacted the water. These concentric circles are more nuanced than the initial splash, but they remain in the water long after the initial splash is gone. Their path of influence covers a much larger area than the initial splash, radiating outward for a much longer period of time.

It is impossible to predict the impact of these concentric circles as they radiate outward across time and space, through different Indigenous territories. *This Is an Honour Song: Twenty Years Since the Blockades* (edited by Kiera Ladner and myself) mapped the multi-generational and trans-national impact of the resistance at Kahnesatà:ke and Kahnawà:ke, otherwise known as the "Oka Crisis." *This Is an Honour Song* demonstrated the positive impact of that act of resistance through time and space. This impact was far reaching and well beyond the intent of the original activists that threw their stone into the lake when they blocked a dirt road leading into the pines that late March morning in 1990. Like the re-creation stories so clearly demonstrate, it is impossible to predict the outcome or influence of a single action or stone's throw once the implicate order is mobilized, and once the act becomes collectivized.

So resurgence starts with individuals aligning themselves within Biskaabiiyang, Naakgonige, Aanjigone and Debwewin. It starts to become osmotically collectivized through our interactions with our families, especially our children, and our communities. And like all Nishnaabeg systems, the processes that guide individual cycles also guide our collective cycles. Decision making within families is mirrored between clans and at the national level. Parenting demonstrates the qualities of leadership, and so on. The family is the microcosm for the nation.

Shki-kiin: New Worlds

In reading John Borrow's *Drawing Out Law: A Spirit's Guide*, and thinking about Maria Campbell's Stone Throw teaching—in addition to thinking about re-creation stories as resurgence—a pattern emerged. Many resurgence or re-creation mobilizations within Nishnaabeg thought starts with a vision or a dream. John Borrows, using Basil Johnston's *Anishinaubae Thesaurus*, terms this "Pauwauwaein," a revelation, an awakening, a vision that gives understanding to matters that were previously obscure.[231] Within our Andizookanan, many, many stories begin with a welcoming of the spirits through a dream: the Creation of the earth itself, the coming of the drum to the Nishnaabeg, and our migration story, to name just a few. When we put our tobacco down and ask for help to solve a problem, to come up with a strategy or so that the Stone we threw ripples through the world in a positive way, we are asking the implicate order to visit our action.

While some stories or mobilizations begin with the gift of knowledge or help from the spiritual world, other stories begin with a vision—a vision of life or a social reality that is different from the one the individual, clan or community is currently living within. Gezhizhwazh visioned a world without Wiindigo. Our Elder Brother visioned a world where the gdigaa bzhiw clan was not lying on their backs drinking maple syrup all day. The young Nishnaabekwe visioned a world in which her small baby was with her and not crying. The act of visioning for Nishnaabeg people is a powerful act of resurgence, because these visions create Shki-kiin, new worlds. Neal McLeod writes, "We must attempt to dream and have visions. Without dreams and idealism, we will truly be a conquered people."[232] Presumably, this is because we will not have the ability to imagine our way out of the cognitive box of imperialism. Presumably, this is because imagining aligns us with the emergent and creative forces of the implicate order.

Because dreams and visions for Nishnaabeg people are spiritual in nature, if one is living in a good way then one becomes open to receiving Pauwauwaewin. But once one has received an important dream, he or she has a responsibility to act on that vision. That responsibility is in essence a treaty we make with the spiritual world when we place our tobacco down and ask for help. Pauwauwaein is an awakening, a vision that gives understanding to matters.[233] Sometimes, the vision is clear and complete, in the case of Pauwauwaewin. Other times, it is incomplete and is a process—an individual might have to speak with an Elder or several Elders in order to understand what that vision means or more ceremonies might be required. More dreams may even be required to understand the meaning. It may take months, years or even decades of searching and learning to fully understand the meaning of one's visions and to chart a course of action. It is the responsibility of the person who had the dream to ensure that the full meaning comes to fruition.

In terms of resurgence, vision alone isn't enough. Vision must be coupled with intent: intent for transformation, intent for re-creation, intent for resurgence. One must have the intention of Biskaabiiyang in order to be effective and to mobilize help from the spirit world. Being ethical about our responsibilities for resurgence within a Nishnaabeg ontology means that we cannot be haphazard about it. Intent matters, and intent is communicated by placing an offering down and asking the implicate order for help.

Naakgonige once again becomes an important process in resurgence as a way of collectivizing, strategizing and making the best decisions possible in any given context. Aanjigone is also important because it ensures that we tread very carefully, to be deliberate to the best of our abilities and that we act out of a tremendous love for our lands, our peoples and our culture. We should do this rather acting than out of responsive anger and criticism, which in themselves are not bad things, but can cloud strategic responses designed to promote more life.

Finally, Skodewin means the art of setting a fire.[234] If you bring Biskaabiiyang, Naakgonige, Aanjigone and Debwewin with intent, vision, motion, emergence, the mobilization of the spiritual world and committed action, one sets a fire. It is a fire that needs to be collectively fed and maintained, grown when it needs to be grown, and reduced to embers at certain times as well, until it is no longer needed for heat, warmth and resilience, and the coals are saved for the next time. To build our fire we need vision, intent, collectivization and action. To promote life, we need the fire within to propel us through the hoops and challenges of resurgence.

Grounding Resurgence in Our Hearts

The volume of teachings, sacred stories, personal narratives and theoretical conceptualizations of "resurgence" within Indigenous thought is tremendous. This book neither represents a comprehensive investigation of these even within one nation, nor does it offer a clear map for Indigenous mobilization. It is a call for Indigenous Peoples to delve into their own culture's stories, philosophies, theories and concepts to align themselves with the processes and forces of regeneration, revitalization, remembering, and visioning. It is a call for Indigenous Peoples to *live* these teachings and stories in the diversity of their contemporary lives, because that act in and of itself is the precursor to generating more stories, processes, visions and forces of regeneration, propelling us into new social spaces based on justice and peace. Our social movements, organizing, and mobilizations are stuck in the cognitive box of imperialism and we need to step out of the box, remove our colonial blinders and at least see the potential for radically different ways of existence. This book is a first step out of that box. Neal McLeod talks about this in terms of tapping into the life force—something that has been present in Cree leaders who move beyond the ordinary:

> Cree narrative imagination can be best articulated by the Cree term *mamâhtâwisiwin*, which could perhaps be best translated as "tapping into the Great Mystery," or "tapping into the Life Force." The term used to describe the elder Brother *wîsahkêcâhk*, *ê-mamâhtâwisit*, was also used to describe *mistahi-maskwa*. All these beings struggled to move beyond the ordinary, and to rethink the space and the world around them.[235]

Regenerating Kina Gchi Nishnaabeg-ogaming requires us to move beyond the ordinary and re-vision the world we currently live in. It requires sacrifice, commitment and countless selfless acts. It requires strategy, commitment and a "one mindedness," built from the diversity of our perspectives and understandings. Our Mothers have always known that our rebirth, like any birth, is a powerful but painful process—a pain that fades into the background as the birthing ceremony comes to an end. Bringing the old into the new is our way forward. This becomes clear when, like Zhaashkoonh, we place our piece on the back of our turtle and dance a new world into existence.

219 Scott Lyons, *X Marks: Native Signatures of Assent*, University of Minnesota Press, Minneapolis, MN, 2010, 84–85.

220 Winona LaDuke, "Minobimaatisiiwin: The Good Life," *Cultural Survival Quarterly*, 16(4): 69–72; and *All Our Relations: Struggles for Land and Life*, South End Press, Cambridge, MA, 1994, 4, 132.

221 I think the process Lyons is going through here is important and similar to the processes that I go through with Elder Doug Williams. Breaking down words reveals deeper conceptual meanings. Observing how these "little" words are used to signify certain attributes in other words shows the expression of that concept through the language. Lyons' interpretations are consistent with John D. Nichols and Earl Nyholm, *A Concise Dictionary of Minnesota Ojibwe*, University of Minnesota Press, Minneapolis, MN, 1995. Scott Lyons, *X Marks: Native Signatures of Assent*, University of Minnesota Press, Minneapolis, MN, 2010, 84–85.

222 Scott Lyons, *X Marks: Native Signatures of Assent*, University of Minnesota Press, Minneapolis, MN, 2010, 85–86.

223 According to John D. Nichols and Earl Nyholm, inaadiziwin means "way of life." *A Concise Dictionary of Minnesota Ojibwe*, University of Minnesota Press, Minneapolis, MN, 1995.

224 Scott Lyons, *X Marks: Native Signatures of Assent*, University of Minnesota Press, Minneapolis, MN, 2010, 86.

225 Scott Lyons, *X Marks: Native Signatures of Assent*, University of Minnesota Press, Minneapolis, MN, 2010, 86.

226 Scott Lyons, *X Marks: Native Signatures of Assent*, University of Minnesota Press, Minneapolis, MN, 2010, 86.

227 According to Nishnaabe language expert Shirley Williams, bimaadiziwin means "the art of life," where as bimaadizi is a verb meaning he/she is alive. Lyons writes that he is concerned that making bimaadizi into a noun, as in bimaadiziwin, is problematic because Nishnaabemowin is a verb-based language and he worries that non fluent speakers are making nouns out of verbs in order to conform to English (see page 88). Shirley Williams explained to me that *bimaadiziwin* as a modified noun was consistent with the traditions and usage of Nishnaabemowin and reflected the correct grammatical usage of the word. She also felt that it still had movement in it. Scott Lyons, *X Marks: Native Signatures of Assent*, University of Minnesota Press, Minneapolis, MN, 2010, 87–88; Shirley Williams, Peterborough, ON, September 12, 2010.

228 Patricia Monture-Angus, *Journeying Forward: Dreaming First Nations Independence*, Fernwood Books, Halifax, NS, 1999, 8.

229 I learned this word from Nishnaabemowin language expert Isadore Toulouse during his online Ojibwe language classes, September 15, 2010.

230 Métis Elder Maria Campbell relayed this to me at Trent University at the book launch for *Lightening the Eighth Fire*, Indigenous Women's Symposium, March 2009. I also used this metaphor in "Niimkiig," Leanne Betasamosake Simpson and Kiera Ladner, eds., *This Is an Honour Song: Twenty Years Since the Blockades*, Arbeiter Ring Publishing, Winnipeg, MB, 2010, 15–23.

231 Basil Johnston, *Anishinaubae Thesaurus*, Michigan State University Press, East Lansing, MI, 2007, 19.

232 Neal McLeod, *Cree Narrative Memory: From Treaties to Contemporary Times*, Purich Press, Saskatoon, SK, 2007, 99.

233 John Borrows, *Drawing Out Law: A Spirit's Guide*, University of Toronto Press, Toronto, ON, 2010, 240, note 1.

234 Basil Johnston states, "Iskugaewin means to kindle, rekindle, to set afire." *Anishinaubae Thesaurus*, Michigan State University Press, East Lansing, MI, 2007, 103. Shirley Williams would use "*Skodewin*" to mean "the art of setting a fire" or *Skage*, "to set a fire," Peterborough, ON, September 12, 2010. Anishinaabe legal scholar John Borrows uses Johnston's translation in *Drawing Out Law: A Spirit's Guide*, University of Toronto Press, Toronto, ON, 2010, 167.

235 Neal McLeod, *Cree Narrative Memory: From Treaties to Contemporary Times*, Purich, Press, Saskatoon, SK, 2007, 100.

INDEX

LEANNE BETASAMOSAKE SIMPSON is a writer, activist, and scholar of Michi Saagiig Nishnaabeg ancestry, with roots in Alderville First Nation. She holds a PhD from the University of Manitoba, is an Adjunct Professor in Indigenous Studies at Trent University and an instructor at the Centre for World Indigenous Knowledge, Athabasca University. She has recently published two edited books, *Lighting the Eighth Fire: The Liberation, Resurgence and Protection of Indigenous Nations* (Arbeiter Ring, 2008), and *This is An Honour Song: Twenty Years Since the Barricades* (with Kiera Ladner, Arbeiter Ring, 2010). Leanne lives in Nogojiwanong with her partner, where she home schools her two children, Nishna and Minowewebeneshiinh. Leanne is currently the co-director of Wii-Kendimiing Nishnaabemowin Saswaansing, a language nest for Nishnaabeg families.